S0-AAF-087

Our Life Together

INSPIRATIONS FOR A LIFETIME

Honor Books
Tulsa, Oklahoma

...ess otherwise indicated, all Scripture quotatio...
...e taken from the *King James Version* of the Bible...

6th Printing
Over 64,000 in Print

Our Life Together
Inspirations for a Lifetime
ISBN 1-56292-751-5
(Formerly ISBN 0-89274-751-X)
Copyright © 1990, 1991 by Honor Books
P. O. Box 55388
Tulsa, Oklahoma 74155

Printed in the United States of America. All right...
reserved under International Copyright Law.
Contents and/or cover may not be reproduced in
whole or in part in any form without the express...
written consent of the Publisher.

Presented To:

_____

By:

_____

_____

Date: _____

Contents

Part II — Devotions for Your Marriage

Part III — Prayers for Your Marriage

Part IV — Selected Poems

Part V — Keys for Success in Marriage

Part VI — Your Marriage Ceremony

Unfeigned Love

The two came together as one in love,
Their hearts knit together by the Father above.

Let no man put asunder what God has ordained . . .
But hold fast forever to this love unfeigned.

— P. Bozorg
— D. Gaines

INTRODUCTION

Your marriage involves more than your wedding and your honeymoon. *Our Life Together* has been created by Honor Books for any stage of your marriage — either the day after the wedding, or your golden anniversary fifty years later. We believe that marriage is not an old-fashioned institution, rather that it is a cornerstone of a healthy society.

Modern society is a hostile environment for marriage, but a marriage built upon the foundation of strong faith and wisdom from the Word of God can endure any climate. The thoughtful and useful features found inside this book will strengthen and encourage you as your marriage grows. Godly counsel, scriptural knowledge and devotional tools are included for you to refer to consistently and confidently.

God's Word for Your Marriage is a collection of scripture promises that God's Word holds for your relationship. There are more than 1,400 scriptures included, covering subjects that range from "God's Plan for Marriage," to "When You Have a Disagreement or Argument." Refer to this section when you need insight on how to deal with a specific situation.

The 30-Day Devotional has been written specifically for couples to use as a tool for a stronger marriage. Successful marriages are built on the Word of God, and here is an easy-to-use format for incorporating it into your daily activities.

Prayers for Your Marriage includes scripturally based prayers for the husband, wife and the relationship. These prayers were written specifically for marriage, and you will find strength and assurance in praying God's Word for your family.

Selected Poems, including ones by Elizabeth Barrett Browning, provide inspiration and joy for your marriage. Timeless favorites, these selections will soon become some of your most treasured poetry.

Six Keys to Marital Happiness by Tim LaHaye is an excerpt from *How To Be Happy Though Married*. The fresh insights and useful wisdom that are written here will serve as a reference section for you to turn to when your life seems to be moving too fast.

Our Life Together is for all married couples. May God bless you as you seek to strengthen your marriage and put Him at the center of your relationship.

Wedding Traditions examines the rich melting pot of cultures that brides and bridegrooms draw from in observing such customs as brides wearing ''Something borrowed, something blue; something old, something new...'' Why and how these and other traditions came into being is explained to help modern couples share a sense of heritage from the very beginning of their life together.

Marriage is meant to last a lifetime.

Part I

God's word for

your marriage

GOD'S PLAN FOR MARRIAGE

And God blessed them, and God said unto them, Be fruitful, and multiply, and replenish the earth, and subdue it: and have dominion over the fish of the sea, and over the fowl of the air, and over every living thing that moveth upon the earth.

Genesis 1:28

And the Lord God said, It is not good that the man should be alone; I will make him an help meet for him.

Genesis 2:18

And the Lord God caused a deep sleep to fall upon Adam, and he slept: and he took one of his ribs, and closed up the flesh instead thereof;

And the rib, which the Lord God had taken from man, made he a woman, and brought her unto the man.

And Adam said, This is now bone of my bones, and flesh of my flesh: she shall be called Woman, because she was taken out of Man.

3

Therefore shall a man leave his father and his mother, and shall cleave unto his wife: and they shall be one flesh.

And they were both naked, the man and his wife, and were not ashamed.

Genesis 2:21-25

House and riches are the inheritance of fathers: and a prudent wife is from the Lord.

Proverbs 19:14

I will therefore that the younger women marry, bear children, guide the house, give none occasion to the adversary to speak reproachfully.

1 Timothy 5:14

Marriage is honourable in all, and the bed undefiled: but whoremongers and adulterers God will judge.

Hebrews 13:4

Nevertheless neither is the man without the woman, neither the woman without the man, in the Lord.

For as the woman is of the man, even so is the man also by the woman; but all things of God.

1 Corinthians 11:11,12

For this cause shall a man leave his father and mother, and shall be joined unto his wife, and they two shall be one flesh.

Ephesians 5:31

Nevertheless, to avoid fornication, let every man have his own wife, and let every woman have her own husband.

Let the husband render unto the wife due benevolence: and likewise also the wife unto the husband.

The wife hath not power of her own body, but the husband: and likewise also the husband hath not power of his own body, but the wife.

Defraud ye not one the other, except it be with consent for a time, that ye may give yourselves to fasting and prayer; and come together again, that Satan tempt you not for your incontinency.
1 Corinthians 7:2-5

And the Pharisees came to him, and asked him, Is it lawful for a man to put away his wife? tempting him.

And he answered and said unto them, What did Moses command you?

And they said, Moses suffered to write a bill of divorcement, and to put her away.

And Jesus answered and said unto them, For the hardness of your heart he wrote you this precept.

But from the beginning of the creation God made them male and female.

For this cause shall a man leave his father and mother, and cleave to his wife.

And they twain shall be one flesh: so then they are no more twain, but one flesh.

What therefore God hath joined together, let not man put asunder.

And in the house his disciples asked him again of the same matter.

And he saith unto them, Whosoever shall put away his wife, and marry another, committeth adultery against her.

And if a woman shall put away her husband, and be married to another, she committeth adultery.

Mark 10:2-12

And he answered and said unto them, Have ye not read, that he which made them at the beginning made them male and female,

And said, For this cause shall a man leave father and mother, and shall cleave to his wife: and they twain shall be one flesh?

Wherefore they are no more twain, but one flesh. What therefore God hath joined together, let not man put asunder.

They say unto him, Why did Moses then command to give a writing of divorcement, and to put her away?

He saith unto them, Moses because of the hardness of your hearts suffered you to put away your wives: but from the beginning it was not so.

And I say unto you, Whosoever shall put away his wife, except it be for fornication, and shall marry another, committeth adultery: and whoso marrieth her which is put away doth commit adultery.

Matthew 19:4-9

Responsibilities
OF THE HUSBAND

Submitting yourselves one to another in the fear of God.

Wives, submit yourselves unto your own husbands, as unto the Lord.

For the husband is the head of the wife, even as Christ is the head of the church: and he is the saviour of the body.

Therefore as the church is subject unto Christ, so let the wives be to their own husbands in every thing.

Husbands, love your wives, even as Christ also loved the church, and gave himself for it.

Ephesians 5:21-25

But I would have you know, that the head of every man is Christ; and the head of the woman is the man; and the head of Christ is God.

1 Corinthians 11:3

For this cause shall a man leave his father and mother, and shall be joined unto his wife, and they two shall be one flesh.

This is a great mystery: but I speak concerning Christ and the church.

Nevertheless let every one of you in particular so love his wife even as himself; and the wife see that she reverence her husband.

Ephesians 5:31-33

Likewise, ye husbands, dwell with them according to knowledge, giving honour unto the wife, as unto the weaker vessel, and as being heirs together of the grace of life; that your prayers be not hindered.

Finally, be ye all of one mind, having compassion one of another, love as brethren, be pitiful, be courteous:

Not rendering evil for evil, or railing for railing: but contrariwise blessing; knowing that ye are thereunto called, that ye should inherit a blessing.

1 Peter 3:7-9

Husbands, love your wives, even as Christ also loved the church, and gave himself for it.

That he might sanctify and cleanse it with the washing of water by the word,

That he might present it to himself a glorious church, not having spot, or wrinkle, or any such thing; but that it should be holy and without blemish.

So ought men to love their wives as their own bodies. He that loveth his wife loveth himself.

For no man ever yet hated his own flesh, but nourisheth and cherisheth it, even as the Lord the church.

Ephesians 5:25-29

Jesus said unto him, Thou shalt love the Lord thy God with all thy heart, and with all thy soul, and with all thy mind.

This is the first and great commandment.

And the second is like unto it, Thou shalt love thy neighbour as thyself.

On these two commandments hang all the law and the prophets.

Matthew 22:37-40

Husbands, love your wives, and be not bitter against them.

Colossians 3:19

Therefore shall a man leave his father and his mother, and shall cleave unto his wife: and they shall be one flesh.

Genesis 2:24

But if any provide not for his own, and specially for those of his own house, he hath denied the faith, and is worse than an infidel.

1 Timothy 5:8

He that troubleth his own house shall inherit the wind: and the fool shall be servant to the wise of heart.

Proverbs 11:29

Let thy fountain be blessed: and rejoice with the wife of thy youth.

Proverbs 5:18

Live joyfully with the wife whom thou lovest all the days of the life of thy vanity, which he hath given thee under the sun, all the days of thy vanity: for that is thy portion in this life, and in thy labour which thou takest under the sun.

Ecclesiastes 9:9

For, brethren, ye have been called unto liberty; only use not liberty for an occasion to the flesh, but by love serve one another.

Galatians 5:13

RESPONSIBILITIES
OF THE WIFE

Submitting yourselves one to another in the fear of God.

Wives, submit yourselves unto your own husbands, as unto the Lord.

For the husband is the head of the wife, even as Christ is the head of the church; and he is the savior of the body.

Therefore, as the church is subject unto Christ, so let wives be to their own husbands in everything.

Ephesians 5:21-24

For this cause shall a man leave his father and mother, and shall be joined unto his wife, and they two shall be one flesh.

This is a great mystery: but I speak concerning Christ and the church.

Nevertheless let every one of you in particular so love his wife even as himself; and the wife see that she reverence her husband.

Ephesians 5:31-33

Let the husband render unto the wife due benevolence: and likewise also the wife unto the husband.

The wife hath not power of her own body, but the husband: and likewise also the husband hath not power of his own body, but the wife.

Defraud ye not one the other, except it be with consent for a time, that ye may give yourselves to fasting and prayer; and come together again, that Satan tempt you not for your incontinency.

1 Corinthians 7:3-5

Jesus said unto him, Thou shalt love the Lord thy God with all thy heart, and with all thy soul, and with all thy mind.

This is the first and great commandment.

And the second is like unto it, Thou shalt love thy neighbour as thyself.

On these two commandments hang all the law and the prophets.

Matthew 22:37-40

Wives, submit yourselves unto your own husbands, as it is fit in the Lord.

Colossians 3:18

Therefore shall a man leave his father and his mother, and shall cleave unto his wife: and they shall be one flesh.

Genesis 2:24

The aged women likewise, that they be in behaviour as becometh holiness, not false accusers, not given to much wine, teachers of good things;

That they may teach the young women to be sober, to love their husbands, to love their children,

To be discreet, chaste, keepers at home, good, obedient to their own husbands, that the word of God be not blasphemed.

Titus 2:3-5

I will therefore that the younger women marry, bear children, guide the house, give none occasion to the adversary to speak reproachfully.

1 Timothy 5:14

For a man indeed ought not to cover his head, forasmuch as he is the image and glory of God: but the woman is the glory of the man.

For the man is not of the woman; but the woman of the man.

Neither was the man created for the woman; but the woman for the man.

1 Corinthians 11:7-9

Who can find a virtuous woman? for her price is far above rubies.

The heart of her husband doth safely trust in her, so that he shall have no need of spoil.

She will do him good and not evil all the days of her life.

She seeketh wool, and flax, and worketh willingly with her hands.

She is like the merchants' ships; she bringeth her food from afar.

She riseth also while it is yet night, and giveth meat to her household, and a portion to her maidens.

She considereth a field, and buyeth it: with the fruit of her hands she planteth a vineyard.

She girdeth her loins with strength, and strengtheneth her arms.

She perceiveth that her merchandise is good: her candle goeth not out by night.

She layeth her hands to the spindle, and her hands hold the distaff.

She stretcheth out her hand to the poor; yea, she reacheth forth her hands to the needy.

She is not afraid of the snow for her household: for all her household are clothed with scarlet.

She maketh herself coverings of tapestry; her clothing is silk and purple.

Her husband is known in the gates, when he sitteth among the elders of the land.

She maketh fine linen, and selleth it; and delivereth girdles unto the merchant.

Strength and honour are her clothing; and she shall rejoice in time to come.

She openeth her mouth with wisdom; and in her tongue is the law of kindness.

She looketh well to the ways of her household, and eateth not the bread of idleness.

Her children arise up, and call her blessed; her husband also, and he praiseth her.

Many daughters have done virtuously, but thou excellest them all.

Favour is deceitful, and beauty is vain: but a woman that feareth the Lord, she shall be praised.

Give her of the fruit of her hands; and let her own works praise her in the gates.

Proverbs 31:10-31

A virtuous woman is a crown to her husband: but she that maketh ashamed is as rottenness in his bones.

Proverbs 12:4

Every wise woman buildeth her house: but the foolish plucketh it down with her hands.

Proverbs 14:1

But I would have you know, that the head of every man is Christ; and the head of the woman is the man; and the head of Christ is God.

1 Corinthians 11:3

Even so must their wives be grave, not slanderers, sober, faithful in all things.

1 Timothy 3:11

As a jewel of gold in a swine's snout, so is a fair woman which is without discretion.

Proverbs 11:22

Unity in Marriage

Can two walk together, except they be agreed?

Amos 3:3

Behold, how good and how pleasant it is for brethren to dwell together in unity!

It is like the precious ointment upon the head, that ran down upon the beard, even Aaron's beard: that went down to the skirts of his garments.

As the dew of Hermon, and as the dew that descended upon the mountains of Zion: for there the Lord commanded the blessing, even life for evermore.

Psalm 133:1-3

And whosoever shall compel thee to go a mile, go with him twain.

Give to him that asketh thee, and from him that would borrow of thee turn not thou away.

Matthew 5:41,42

This is my commandment, That ye love one another, as I have loved you.

Greater love hath no man than this, that a man lay down his life for his friends.

John 15:12,13

Let love be without dissimulation. Abhor that which is evil; cleave to that which is good.

Be kindly affectioned one to another with brotherly love; in honour preferring one another.

Romans 12:9,10

And walk in love, as Christ also hath loved us, and hath given himself for us an offering and a sacrifice to God for a sweetsmelling savour.

Ephesians 5:2

Put on therefore, as the elect of God, holy and beloved, bowels of mercies, kindness, humbleness of mind, meekness, longsuffering.

Forbearing one another, and forgiving one another, if any man have a quarrel against any: even as Christ forgave you, so also do ye.

And above all these things put on charity, which is the bond of perfectness.

Colossians 3:12-14

And the Lord make you to increase and abound in love one toward another, and toward all men, even as we do toward you.

1 Thessalonians 3:12

And let us consider one another to provoke unto love and to good works.

Hebrews 10:24

Be of the same mind one toward another. Mind not high things, but condescend to men of low estate. Be not wise in your own conceits.

Romans 12:16

Let us therefore follow after the things which make for peace, and things wherewith one may edify another.

Romans 14:19

Now the God of patience and consolation grant you to be likeminded one toward another according to Christ Jesus:

That ye may with one mind and one mouth glorify God, even the Father of our Lord Jesus Christ.

Romans 15:5,6

Now I beseech you, brethren, by the name of our Lord Jesus Christ, that ye all speak the same thing, and that there be no divisions among you; but that ye be perfectly joined together in the same mind and in the same judgment.

1 Corinthians 1:10

Finally, brethren, farewell. Be perfect, be of good comfort, be of one mind, live in peace; and the God of love and peace shall be with you.

2 Corinthians 13:11

Fulfil ye my joy, that ye be likeminded, having the same love, being of one accord, of one mind.

Philippians 2:2

Finally, be ye all of one mind, having compassion one of another, love as brethren, be pitiful, be courteous.

1 Peter 3:8

Endeavouring to keep the unity of the Spirit in the bond of peace.

Ephesians 4:3

Only let your conversation be as it becometh the gospel of Christ: that whether I come and see you, or else be absent, I may hear of your affairs, that ye stand fast in one spirit, with one mind striving together for the faith of the gospel.

Philippians 1:27

Two are better than one; because they have a good reward for their labour.

Ecclesiastes 4:9

And if one prevail against him, two shall withstand him; and a threefold cord is not quickly broken.

Ecclesiastes 4:12

Dealing with Parents and In-Laws

For this cause shall a man leave his father and mother, and cleave to his wife;

And they twain shall be one flesh: so then they are no more twain, but one flesh.

Mark 10:7,8

Honour thy father and mother; which is the first commandment with promise.

That it may be well with thee, and thou mayest live long on the earth.

Ephesians 6:2,3

A wise son heareth his father's instruction: but a scorner heareth not rebuke.

Proverbs 13:1

My son, hear the instruction of thy father, and forsake not the law of thy mother:

For they shall be an ornament of grace unto thy head, and chains about thy neck.

Proverbs 1:8,9

Be kindly affectioned one to another with brotherly love; in honour preferring one another.

Romans 12:10

Let nothing be done through strife or vainglory; but in lowliness of mind let each esteem other better than themselves.

Philippians 2:3

He that wasteth his father, and chaseth away his mother, is a son that causeth shame, and bringeth reproach.

Proverbs 19:26

Hearken unto thy father that begat thee, and despise not thy mother when she is old.

Proverbs 23:22

Therefore shall a man leave his father and his mother, and shall cleave unto his wife: and they shall be one flesh.

Genesis 2:24

The eye that mocketh at his father, and despiseth to obey his mother, the ravens of the valley shall pick it out, and the young eagles shall eat it.

Proverbs 30:17

For God commanded, saying, Honour thy father and mother: and, He that curseth father or mother, let him die the death.

Matthew 15:4

For this cause shall a man leave his father and mother, and shall be joined unto his wife, and they two shall be one flesh.

Ephesians 5:31

Rebuke not an elder, but intreat him as a father; and the younger men as brethren.

1 Timothy 5:1

Honour thy father and thy mother, as the Lord thy God hath commanded thee; that thy days may be prolonged, and that it may go well with thee, in the land which the Lord thy God giveth thee.

Deuteronomy 5:16

Charity suffereth long, and is kind; charity envieth not; charity vaunteth not itself, is not puffed up,

Doth not behave itself unseemly, seeketh not her own, is not easily provoked, thinketh no evil.

Rejoiceth not in iniquity, but rejoiceth in the truth.

Beareth all things, believeth all things, hopeth all things, endureth all things.

Charity never faileth: but whether there be prophecies, they shall fail; whether there be tongues, they shall cease; whether there be knowledge, it shall vanish away.

1 Corinthians 13:4-8

GOD'S FAVOR IN MARRIAGE

Whoso findeth a wife findeth a good thing, and obtaineth favour of the Lord.

Proverbs 18:22

He that diligently seeketh good procureth favour: but he that seeketh mischief, it shall come unto him.

Proverbs 11:27

A good man obtaineth favour of the Lord: but a man of wicked devices will he condemn.

Proverbs 12:2

Let not mercy and truth forsake thee: bind them about thy neck; write them upon the table of thine heart:
So shalt thou find favour and good understanding in the sight of God and man.

Proverbs 3:3,4

For thou, Lord, wilt bless the righteous; with favour wilt thou compass him as with a shield.

Psalm 5:12

Good understanding giveth favour: but the way of transgressors is hard.

Proverbs 13:15

Fools make a mock at sin: but among the righteous there is favour.

Proverbs 14:9

Thy wife shall be as a fruitful vine by the sides of thine house: thy children like olive plants round about thy table.

Behold, that thus shall the man be blessed that feareth the Lord.

Psalm 128:3,4

Now when the turn of Esther, the daughter of Abihail the uncle of Mordecai, who had taken her for his daughter, was come to go in unto the king, she required nothing but what Hegai the king's chamberlain, the keeper of the women, appointed. And Esther obtained favour in the sight of all them that looked upon her.

Esther 2:15

And the king loved Esther above all the women, and she obtained grace and favour in his sight more than all the virgins; so that he set the royal crown upon her head, and made her queen instead of Vashti.

Esther 2:17

And it was so, when the king saw Esther the queen standing in the court, that she obtained favour in his sight: and the king held out to Esther the golden sceptre that was in his hand.

Esther 5:2

Thou hast granted me life and favour, and thy visitation hath preserved my spirit.

Job 10:12

For his anger endureth but a moment; in his favour is life: weeping may endure for a night, but joy cometh in the morning.

Psalm 30:5

Remember me, O Lord, with the favour that thou bearest unto thy people: O visit me with thy salvation.

Psalm 106:4

A good man sheweth favour, and lendeth: he will guide his affairs with discretion.

Psalm 112:5

Good understanding giveth favour: but the way of transgressors is hard.

Proverbs 13:15

WALKING IN LOVE

Hatred stirreth up strifes: but love covereth all sins.

Proverbs 10:12

Many waters cannot quench love, neither can the floods drown it: if a man would give all the substance of his house for love, it would utterly be contemned.

Song of Solomon 8:7

A new commandment I give unto you, That ye love one another; as I have loved you, that ye also love one another.

By this shall all men know that ye are my disciples, if ye have love one to another.

John 13:34,35

Owe no man any thing, but to love one another: for he that loveth another hath fulfilled the law.

For this, Thou shalt not commit adultery, Thou shalt not kill, Thou shalt not steal, Thou shalt not bear false witness, Thou shalt not covet; and if there be any other commandment, it is briefly comprehended in this saying, namely, Thou shalt love thy neighbour as thyself.

Love worketh no ill to his neighbour: therefore love is the fulfilling of the law.

Romans 13:8-10

Be ye therefore followers of God, as dear children;

And walk in love, as Christ also hath loved us, and hath given himself for us an offering and a sacrifice to God for a sweetsmelling savour.

Ephesians 5:1,2

Though I speak with the tongues of men and of angels, and have not charity, I am become as sounding brass, or a tinkling cymbal.

And though I have the gift of prophecy, and understand all mysteries, and all knowledge; and though I have all faith, so that I could remove mountains, and have not charity, I am nothing.

And though I bestow all my goods to feed the poor, and though I give my body to be burned, and have not charity, it profiteth me nothing.

Charity suffereth long, and is kind; charity envieth not; charity vaunteth not itself, is not puffed up,

Doth not behave itself unseemly, seeketh not her own, is not easily provoked, thinketh no evil;

Rejoiceth not in iniquity, but rejoiceth in the truth;

Beareth all things, believeth all things, hopeth all things, endureth all things.

Charity never faileth: but whether there be prophecies, they shall fail; whether there be tongues, they shall cease; whether there be knowledge, it shall vanish away.

For we know in part, and we prophesy in part.

But when that which is perfect is come, then that which is in part shall be done away.

When I was a child, I spake as a child, I understood as a child, I thought as a child: but when I became a man, I put away childish things.

For now we see through a glass, darkly; but then face to face: now I know in part; but then shall I know even as also I am known.

And now abideth faith, hope, charity, these three; but the greatest of these is charity.

1 Corinthians 13:1-13

And the Lord make you to increase and abound in love one toward another, and toward all men, even as we do toward you:

1 Thessalonians 3:12

As the Father hath loved me, so have I loved you: continue ye in my love.

If ye keep my commandments, ye shall abide in my love; even as I have kept my Father's commandments, and abide in his love.

John 15:9,10

This is my commandment, That ye love one another, as I have loved you.

Greater love hath no man than this, that a man lay down his life for his friends.

Ye are my friends, if ye do whatsoever I command you.

Henceforth I call you not servants; for the servant knoweth not what his lord doeth: but I have called you friends; for all things that I have heard of my Father I have made known unto you.

Ye have not chosen me, but I have chosen you, and ordained you, that ye should go and bring forth fruit, and that your fruit should remain: that whatsoever ye shall ask of the Father in my name, he may give it you.

These things I command you, that ye love one another.

John 15:12-17

And let us consider one another to provoke unto love and to good works.

Hebrews 10:24

If ye fulfil the royal law according to the scripture, Thou shalt love thy neighbour as thyself, ye do well.

James 2:8

For this is the message that ye heard from the beginning, that we should love one another.

1 John 3:11

We know that we have passed from death unto life, because we love the brethren. He that loveth not his brother abideth in death.

Whosoever hateth his brother is a murderer: and ye know that no murderer hath eternal life abiding in him.

Hereby perceive we the love of God, because he laid down his life for us: and we ought to lay down our lives for the brethren.

1 John 3:14-16

Beloved, let us love one another: for love is of God; and every one that loveth is born of God, and knoweth God.

He that loveth not knoweth not God; for God is love.

1 John 4:7,8

And above all things have fervent charity among yourselves: for charity shall cover the multitude of sins.

1 Peter 4:8

Finally, be ye all of one mind, having compassion one of another, love as brethren, be pitiful, be courteous.

1 Peter 3:8

Put on therefore, as the elect of God, holy and beloved, bowels of mercies, kindness, humbleness of mind, meekness, longsuffering.

Forbearing one another, and forgiving one another, if any man have a quarrel against any: even as Christ forgave you, so also do ye.

And above all these things put on charity, which is the bond of perfectness.

Colossians 3:12-14

He that covereth a transgression seeketh love; but he that repeateth a matter separateth very friends.

Proverbs 17:9

But thou, O man of God, flee these things; and follow after righteousness, godliness, faith, love, patience, meekness.

1 Timothy 6:11

Let love be without dissimulation. Abhor that which is evil; cleave to that which is good.

Be kindly affectioned one to another with brotherly love; in honour preferring one another.

Romans 12:9,10

For, brethren, ye have been called unto liberty; only use not liberty for an occasion to the flesh, but by love serve one another.

Galatians 5:13

LISTENING TO YOUR SPOUSE

Beloved, let us love one another: for love is of God; and every one that loveth is born of God, and knoweth God.

He that loveth not knoweth not God; for God is love.

1 John 4:7,8

The way of a fool is right in his own eyes: but he that hearkeneth unto counsel is wise.

Proverbs 12:15

Only by pride cometh contention: but with the well advised is wisdom.

Proverbs 13:10

Wherefore, my beloved brethren, let every man be swift to hear, slow to speak, slow to wrath:

For the wrath of man worketh not the righteousness of God.

James 1:19,20

The heart of the prudent getteth knowledge; and the ear of the wise seeketh knowledge.

Proverbs 18:15

A wise man will hear, and will increase learning; and a man of understanding shall attain unto wise counsels:

Proverbs 1:5

My son, hear the instruction of thy father, and forsake not the law of thy mother:

For they shall be an ornament of grace unto thy head, and chains about thy neck.

Proverbs 1:8,9

The ear that heareth the reproof of life abideth among the wise.

Proverbs 15:31

Hear instruction, and be wise, and refuse it not.

Blessed is the man that heareth me, watching daily at my gates, waiting at the posts of my doors.

For whoso findeth me findeth life, and shall obtain favour of the Lord.

Proverbs 8:33-35

Whoso loveth instruction loveth knowledge: but he that hateth reproof is brutish.

Proverbs 12:1

But blessed are your eyes, for they see: and your ears, for they hear.

Matthew 13:16

A fool uttereth all his mind: but a wise man keepeth it in till afterwards.

Proverbs 29:11

THE WORDS OF YOUR MOUTH

Not rendering evil for evil, or railing for railing: but contrariwise blessing; knowing that ye are thereunto called, that ye should inherit a blessing.

For he that will love life, and see good days, let him refrain his tongue from evil, and his lips that they speak no guile.

1 Peter 3:9,10

And let us consider one another to provoke unto love and to good works.

Hebrews 10:24

He that speaketh truth sheweth forth righteousness: but a false witness deceit.

There is that speaketh like the piercings of a sword: but the tongue of the wise is health.

The lip of truth shall be established for ever: but a lying tongue is but for a moment.

Proverbs 12:17-19

Lying lips are abomination to the Lord: but they that deal truly are his delight.

A prudent man concealeth knowledge: but the heart of fools proclaimeth foolishness.

Proverbs 12:22,23

Heaviness in the heart of man maketh it stoop: but a good word maketh it glad.

Proverbs 12:25

He that keepeth his mouth keepeth his life: but he that openeth wide his lips shall have destruction.

Proverbs 13:3

The heart of him that hath understanding seeketh knowledge: but the mouth of fools feedeth on foolishness.

Proverbs 15:14

A soft answer turneth away wrath: but grievous words stir up anger.

The tongue of the wise useth knowledge aright: but the mouth of fools poureth out foolishness.

Proverbs 15:1,2

A wholesome tongue is a tree of life: but perverseness therein is a breach in the spirit.

Proverbs 15:4

A man hath joy by the answer of his mouth: and a word spoken in due season, how good is it!

Proverbs 15:23

The thoughts of the wicked are an abomination to the Lord: but the words of the pure are pleasant words.

Proverbs 15:26

The light of the eyes rejoiceth the heart: and a good report maketh the bones fat.

Proverbs 15:30

Keep thy tongue from evil, and thy lips from speaking guile.

Psalm 34:13

Pleasant words are as an honeycomb, sweet to the soul, and health to the bones.

Proverbs 16:24

He that hath a froward heart findeth no good: and he that hath a perverse tongue falleth into mischief.

Proverbs 17:20

He that hath knowledge spareth his words: and a man of understanding is of an excellent spirit.

Proverbs 17:27

A fool's lips enter into contention, and his mouth calleth for strokes.

A fool's mouth is his destruction, and his lips are the snare of his soul.

The words of a talebearer are as wounds, and they go down into the innermost parts of the belly.

Proverbs 18:6-8

Death and life are in the power of the tongue: and they that love it shall eat the fruit thereof.

Proverbs 18:21

O generation of vipers, how can ye, being evil, speak good things? for out of the abundance of the heart the mouth speaketh.

Matthew 12:34

Wherefore, my beloved brethren, let every man be swift to hear, slow to speak, slow to wrath:

For the wrath of man worketh not the righteousness of God.

James 1:19,20

Let no corrupt communication proceed out of your mouth, but that which is good to the use of edifying, that it may minister grace unto the hearers.

Ephesians 4:29

Let all bitterness, and wrath, and anger, and clamour, and evil speaking, be put away from you, with all malice.

Ephesians 4:31

To speak evil of no man, to be no brawlers, but gentle, shewing all meekness unto all men.

Titus 3:2

Wherefore laying aside all malice, and all guile, and hypocrisies, and envies, and all evil speakings.

1 Peter 2:1

If any man among you seem to be religious, and bridleth not his tongue, but deceiveth his own heart, this man's religion is vain.

James 1:26

Let your speech be alway with grace, seasoned with salt, that ye may know how ye ought to answer every man.

Colossians 4:6

The mouth of the righteous speaketh wisdom, and his tongue talketh of judgment.

Psalm 37:30

My mouth shall speak of wisdom; and the meditation of my heart shall be of understanding.

Psalm 49:3

The mouth of the just bringeth forth wisdom: but the froward tongue shall be cut out.

Proverbs 10:31

A fool uttereth all his mind: but a wise man keepeth it in till afterwards.

Proverbs 29:11

But I say unto you, That every idle word that men shall speak, they shall give account thereof in the day of judgment.

For by thy words thou shalt be justified, and by thy words thou shalt be condemned.

Matthew 12:36,37

ENCOURAGING YOUR SPOUSE

But exhort one another daily, while it is called To day; lest any of you be hardened through the deceitfulness of sin.

Hebrews 3:13

And let us consider one another to provoke unto love and to good works.

Hebrews 10:24

Let us therefore follow after the things which make for peace, and things wherewith one may edify another.

Romans 14:19

We then that are strong ought to bear the infirmities of the weak, and not to please ourselves.

Let every one of us please his neighbour for his good to edification.

Romans 15:1,2

Bear ye one another's burdens, and so fulfil the law of Christ.

Galatians 6:2

Wherefore comfort yourselves together, and edify one another, even as also ye do.

1 Thessalonians 5:11

And this I pray, that your love may abound yet more and more in knowledge and in all judgment.

Philippians 1:9

Furthermore then we beseech you, brethren, and exhort you by the Lord Jesus, that as ye have received of us how ye ought to walk and to please God, so ye would abound more and more.

1 Thessalonians 4:1

Let love be without dissimulation. Abhor that which is evil; cleave to that which is good.
Be kindly affectioned one to another with brotherly love; in honour preferring one another.

Romans 12:9,10

My little children, let us not love in word, neither in tongue; but in deed and in truth.

1 John 3:18

Put on therefore, as the elect of God, holy and beloved, bowels of mercies, kindness, humbleness of mind, meekness, longsuffering;
Forbearing one another, and forgiving one another, if any man have a quarrel against any: even as Christ forgave you, so also do ye.

Colossians 3:12,13

Ye shall not therefore oppress one another; but thou shalt fear thy God: for I am the Lord your God.

Leviticus 25:17

Blessed be God, even the Father of our Lord Jesus Christ, the Father of mercies, and the God of all comfort;

Who comforteth us in all our tribulation, that we may be able to comfort them which are in any trouble, by the comfort wherewith we ourselves are comforted of God.

2 Corinthians 1:3,4

There is therefore now no condemnation to them which are in Christ Jesus, who walk not after the flesh, but after the Spirit.

Romans 8:1

Finally, my brethren, be strong in the Lord, and in the power of his might.

Put on the whole armour of God, that ye may be able to stand against the wiles of the devil.

Ephesians 6:10,11

Be careful for nothing; but in every thing by prayer and supplication with thanksgiving let your requests be made known unto God.

And the peace of God, which passeth all understanding, shall keep your hearts and minds through Christ Jesus.

Philippians 4:6,7

Finally, brethren, farewell. Be perfect, be of good comfort, be of one mind, live in peace; and the God of love and peace shall be with you.

2 Corinthians 13:11

Sing, O heavens; and be joyful, O earth; and break forth into singing, O mountains: for the Lord hath comforted his people, and will have mercy upon his afflicted.

Isaiah 49:13

Now our Lord Jesus Christ himself, and God, even our Father, which hath loved us, and hath given us everlasting consolation and good hope through grace,

Comfort your hearts, and stablish you in every good word and work.

2 Thessalonians 2:16,17

For we have not an high priest which cannot be touched with the feeling of our infirmities; but was in all points tempted like as we are, yet without sin.

Let us therefore come boldly unto the throne of grace, that we may obtain mercy, and find grace to help in time of need.

Hebrews 4:15,16

Finally, be ye all of one mind, having compassion one of another, love as brethren, be pitiful, be courteous.

1 Peter 3:8

DEALING WITH CRITICISM

So that we may boldly say, The Lord is my helper, and I will not fear what man shall do unto me.

Hebrews 13:6

Be not overcome of evil, but overcome evil with good.

Romans 12:21

The words of a talebearer are as wounds, and they go down into the innermost parts of the belly.

Proverbs 18:8

He that goeth about as a talebearer revealeth secrets: therefore meddle not with him that flattereth with his lips.

Proverbs 20:19

A froward man soweth strife: and a whisperer separateth chief friends.

Proverbs 16:28

Where no wood is, there the fire goeth out: so where there is no talebearer, the strife ceaseth.

As coals are to burning coals, and wood to fire; so is a contentious man to kindle strife.

The words of a talebearer are as wounds, and they go down into the innermost parts of the belly.

Proverbs 26:20-22

Put on therefore, as the elect of God, holy and beloved, bowels of mercies, kindness, humbleness of mind, meekness, longsuffering;

Forbearing one another, and forgiving one another, if any man have a quarrel against any: even as Christ forgave you, so also do ye.

Colossians 3:12,13

Judge not, and ye shall not be judged: condemn not, and ye shall not be condemned: forgive, and ye shall be forgiven:

Give, and it shall be given unto you; good measure, pressed down, and shaken together, and running over, shall men give into your bosom. For with the same measure that ye mete withal it shall be measured to you again.

Luke 6:37,38

Beloved, let us love one another: for love is of God; and every one that loveth is born of God, and knoweth God.

He that loveth not knoweth not God; for God is love.

1 John 4:7,8

Herein is love, not that we loved God, but that he loved us, and sent his Son to be the propitiation for our sins.

Beloved, if God so loved us, we ought also to love one another.

No man hath seen God at any time. If we love one another, God dwelleth in us, and his love is perfected in us.

1 John 4:10-12

And we have known and believed the love that God hath to us. God is love; and he that dwelleth in love dwelleth in God, and God in him.

1 John 4:16

And this commandment have we from him, That he who loveth God love his brother also.
1 John 4:21

Blessed are ye, when men shall revile you, and persecute you, and shall say all manner of evil against you falsely, for my sake.

Rejoice, and be exceeding glad: for great is your reward in heaven: for so persecuted they the prophets which were before you.
Matthew 5:11,12

If ye be reproached for the name of Christ, happy are ye; for the spirit of glory and of God resteth upon you: on their part he is evil spoken of, but on your part he is glorified.

1 Peter 4:14

He shall send from heaven, and save me from the reproach of him that would swallow me up. Selah. God shall send forth his mercy and his truth.

Psalm 57:3

Hearken unto me, ye that know righteousness, the people in whose heart is my law; fear ye not the reproach of men, neither be ye afraid of their revilings.

Isaiah 51:7

Judge not, that ye be not judged.

For with what judgment ye judge, ye shall be judged: and with what measure ye mete, it shall be measured to you again.

And why beholdest thou the mote that is in thy brother's eye, but considerest not the beam that is in thine own eye?

Or how wilt thou say to thy brother, Let me pull out the mote out of thine eye; and, behold, a beam is in thine own eye?

Thou hypocrite, first cast out the beam out of thine own eye; and then shalt thou see clearly to cast out the mote out of thy brother's eye.

Matthew 7:1-5

Judge not according to the appearance, but judge righteous judgment.

John 7:24

So when they continued asking him, he lifted up himself, and said unto them, He that is without sin among you, let him first cast a stone at her.

John 8:7

Therefore thou art inexcusable, O man, whosoever thou art that judgest: for wherein thou judgest another, thou condemnest thyself; for thou that judgest doest the same things.

Romans 2:1

Keep thy tongue from evil, and thy lips from speaking guile.

Psalm 34:13

Put away from thee a froward mouth, and perverse lips put far from thee.

Proverbs 4:24

He that keepeth his mouth keepeth his life: but he that openeth wide his lips shall have destruction.

Proverbs 13:3

A wholesome tongue is a tree of life: but perverseness therein is a breach in the spirit.

Proverbs 15:4

To speak evil of no man, to be no brawlers, but gentle, shewing all meekness unto all men.

Titus 3:2

DISAGREEMENTS/ARGUMENTS

And above all things have fervent charity among yourselves: for charity shall cover the multitude of sins.

1 Peter 4:8

A soft answer turneth away wrath: but grievous words stir up anger.

The tongue of the wise useth knowledge aright: but the mouth of fools poureth out foolishness.

Proverbs 15:1,2

Can two walk together, except they be agreed?

Amos 3:3

Wherefore, my beloved brethren, let every man be swift to hear, slow to speak, slow to wrath:

For the wrath of man worketh not the righteousness of God.

James 1:19,20

Be not hasty in thy spirit to be angry: for anger resteth in the bosom of fools.

Ecclesiastes 7:9

A wise man feareth, and departeth from evil: but the fool rageth, and is confident.

He that is soon angry dealeth foolishly: and a man of wicked devices is hated.

Proverbs 14:16,17

He that is slow to anger is better than the mighty; and he that ruleth his spirit than he that taketh a city.

Proverbs 16:32

A wrathful man stirreth up strife: but he that is slow to anger appeaseth strife.

Proverbs 15:18

An angry man stirreth up strife, and a furious man aboundeth in transgression.

Proverbs 29:22

Cease from anger, and forsake wrath: fret not thyself in any wise to do evil.

Psalm 37:8

Be ye angry, and sin not: let not the sun go down upon your wrath.

Ephesians 4:26

The discretion of a man deferreth his anger; and it is his glory to pass over a transgression.

Proverbs 19:11

Let all bitterness, and wrath, and anger, and clamour, and evil speaking, be put away from you, with all malice:

And be ye kind one to another, tender-hearted, forgiving one another, even as God for Christ's sake hath forgiven you.

Ephesians 4:31,32

Dearly beloved, avenge not yourselves, but rather give place unto wrath: for it is written, Vengeance is mine; I will repay, saith the Lord.

Therefore if thine enemy hunger, feed him; if he thirst, give him drink: for in so doing thou shalt heap coals of fire on his head.

Be not overcome of evil, but overcome evil with good.

Romans 12:19-21

But now ye also put off all these; anger, wrath, malice, blasphemy, filthy communication out of your mouth.

Colossians 3:8

He that is slow to wrath is of great understanding: but he that is hasty of spirit exalteth folly.

Proverbs 14:29

For God is not the author of confusion, but of peace, as in all churches of the saints.

1 Corinthians 14:33

Finally, be ye all of one mind, having compassion one of another, love as brethren, be pitiful, be courteous:

Not rendering evil for evil, or railing for railing: but contrariwise blessing; knowing that ye are thereunto called, that ye should inherit a blessing.

For he that will love life, and see good days, let him refrain his tongue from evil, and his lips that they speak no guile:

Let him eschew evil, and do good; let him seek peace, and ensue it.

1 Peter 3:8-11

Honesty

He that speaketh truth sheweth forth
righteousness: but a false witness deceit.

Proverbs 12:17

Lying lips are abomination to the Lord: but
they that deal truly are his delight.

Proverbs 12:22

A righteous man hateth lying: but a wicked
man is loathsome, and cometh to shame.

Proverbs 13:5

A faithful witness will not lie: but a false
witness will utter lies.

Proverbs 14:5

A false witness shall not be unpunished, and
he that speaketh lies shall perish.

Proverbs 19:9

And that ye put on the new man, which after
God is created in righteousness and true
holiness.

Wherefore putting away lying, speak every
man truth with his neighbour: for we are
members one of another.

Ephesians 4:24,25

Recompense to no man evil for evil. Provide things honest in the sight of all men.

Romans 12:17

Finally, brethren, whatsoever things are true, whatsoever things are honest, whatsoever things are just, whatsoever things are pure, whatsoever things are lovely, whatsoever things are of good report; if there be any virtue, and if there be any praise, think on these things.

Philippians 4:8

Having your conversation honest among the Gentiles: that, whereas they speak against you as evildoers, they may by your good works, which they shall behold, glorify God in the day of visitation.

1 Peter 2:12

The integrity of the upright shall guide them: but the perverseness of transgressors shall destroy them.

Proverbs 11:3

He that hath clean hands, and a pure heart; who hath not lifted up his soul unto vanity, nor sworn deceitfully.

He shall receive the blessing from the Lord, and righteousness from the God of his salvation.

Psalm 24:4,5

But have renounced the hidden things of dishonesty, not walking in craftiness, nor handling the word of God deceitfully; but by manifestation of the truth commending ourselves to every man's conscience in the sight of God.

2 Corinthians 4:2

But speaking the truth in love, may grow up into him in all things, which is the head, even Christ.

Ephesians 4:15

Behold, thou desirest truth in the inward parts: and in the hidden part thou shalt make me to know wisdom.

Psalm 51:6

For my mouth shall speak truth; and wickedness is an abomination to my lips.

Proverbs 8:7

He that saith, I know him, and keepeth not his commandments, is a liar, and the truth is not in him.

1 John 2:4

Lead me in thy truth, and teach me: for thou art the God of my salvation; on thee do I wait all the day.

Psalm 25:5

Providing for honest things, not only in the sight of the Lord, but also in the sight of men.

2 Corinthians 8:21

Ye shall not steal, neither deal falsely, neither lie one to another.

Leviticus 19:11

Lie not one to another, seeing that ye have put off the old man with his deeds.

And have put on the new man, which is renewed in knowledge after the image of him that created him.

Colossians 3:9,10

And herein do I exercise myself, to have always a conscience void of offence toward God, and toward men.

Acts 24:16

The law of truth was in his mouth, and iniquity was not found in his lips: he walked with me in peace and equity, and did turn many away from iniquity.

Malachi 2:6

That which is altogether just shalt thou follow, that thou mayest live, and inherit the land which the Lord thy God giveth thee.

Deuteronomy 16:20

And as ye would that men should do to you, do ye also to them likewise.

Luke 6:31

And that ye study to be quiet, and to do your own business, and to work with your own hands, as we commanded you.

1 Thessalonians 4:11

Let the lying lips be put to silence; which speak grievous things proudly and contemptuously against the righteous.

Psalm 31:18

Ye shall not steal, neither deal falsely, neither lie one to another.

Leviticus 19:11

Now the Spirit speaketh expressly, that in the latter times some shall depart from the faith, giving heed to seducing spirits, and doctrines of devils.

Speaking lies in hypocrisy; having their conscience seared with a hot iron.

1 Timothy 4:1,2

But the king shall rejoice in God; every one that sweareth by him shall glory: but the mouth of them that speak lies shall be stopped.

Psalm 63:11

Let not mercy and truth forsake thee: bind them about thy neck; write them upon the table of thine heart.

Proverbs 3:3

DEALING WITH
STRIFE/CONTENTIONS

It is better to dwell in a corner of the housetop, than with a brawling woman in a wide house.

Proverbs 21:9

It is better to dwell in the wilderness, than with a contentious and an angry woman.

Proverbs 21:19

Hatred stirreth up strifes: but love covereth all sins.

Proverbs 10:12

And let us consider one another to provoke unto love and to good works.

Hebrews 10:24

And above all things have fervent charity among yourselves: for charity shall cover the multitude of sins.

1 Peter 4:8

Only by pride cometh contention: but with the well advised is wisdom.

Proverbs 13:10

A foolish son is the calamity of his father: and the contentions of a wife are a continual dropping.

Proverbs 19:13

A soft answer turneth away wrath: but grievous words stir up anger.

The tongue of the wise useth knowledge aright: but the mouth of fools poureth out foolishness.

Proverbs 15:1,2

A fool's lips enter into contention, and his mouth calleth for strokes.

Proverbs 18:6

Better is a dry morsel, and quietness therewith, than an house full of sacrifices with strife.

Proverbs 17:1

But if ye have bitter envying and strife in your hearts, glory not, and lie not against the truth.

James 3:14

The beginning of strife is as when one letteth out water: therefore leave off contention, before it be meddled with.

Proverbs 17:14

He loveth transgression that loveth strife: and he that exalteth his gate seeketh destruction.

Proverbs 17:19

The discretion of a man deferreth his anger; and it is his glory to pass over a transgression.

Proverbs 19:11

Blessed are the peacemakers: for they shall be called the children of God.

Matthew 5:9

Be ye angry, and sin not: let not the sun go down upon your wrath.

Ephesians 4:26

Let all bitterness, and wrath, and anger, and clamour, and evil speaking, be put away from you, with all malice.

Ephesians 4:31

And let us consider one another to provoke unto love and to good works.

Hebrews 10:24

For where envying and strife is, there is confusion and every evil work.

James 3:16

Hatred stirreth up strifes: but love covereth all sins.

Proverbs 10:12

Can two walk together, except they be agreed?

Amos 3:3

Strive not with a man without cause, if he have done thee no harm.

Proverbs 3:30

He that is slow to wrath is of great understanding: but he that is hasty of spirit exalteth folly.

Proverbs 14:29

Let nothing be done through strife or vainglory; but in lowliness of mind let each esteem other better than themselves.

Philippians 2:3

It is an honour for a man to cease from strife: but every fool will be meddling.

Proverbs 20:3

Go not forth hastily to strive, lest thou know not what to do in the end thereof, when thy neighbour hath put thee to shame.

Proverbs 25:8

He that passeth by, and meddleth with strife belonging not to him, is like one that taketh a dog by the ears.

Proverbs 26:17

Of these things put them in remembrance, charging them before the Lord that they strive not about words to no profit, but to the subverting of the hearers.

2 Timothy 2:14

And the servant of the Lord must not strive; but be gentle unto all men, apt to teach, patient,

In meekness instructing those that oppose themselves; if God peradventure will give them repentance to the acknowledging of the truth.

2 Timothy 2:24,25

A brother offended is harder to be won than a strong city: and their contentions are like the bars of a castle.

Proverbs 18:19

A continual dropping in a very rainy day and a contentious woman are alike.

Proverbs 27:15

A wrathful man stirreth up strife: but he that is slow to anger appeaseth strife.

Proverbs 15:18

As coals are to burning coals, and wood to fire; so is a contentious man to kindle strife.

Proverbs 26:21

A wrathful man stirreth up strife: but he that is slow to anger appeaseth strife.

Proverbs 15:18

DEALING WITH REJECTION

Behold, what manner of love the Father hath bestowed upon us, that we should be called the sons of God: therefore the world knoweth us not, because it knew him not.

1 John 3:1

For we have not an high priest which cannot be touched with the feeling of our infirmities; but was in all points tempted like as we are, yet without sin.

Let us therefore come boldly unto the throne of grace, that we may obtain mercy, and find grace to help in time of need.

Hebrews 4:15,16

A man that hath friends must shew himself friendly: and there is a friend that sticketh closer than a brother.

Proverbs 18:24

The righteous cry, and the Lord heareth, and delivereth them out of all their troubles.

The Lord is nigh unto them that are of a broken heart; and saveth such as be of a contrite spirit.

Psalm 34:17,18

What shall we then say to these things? If God be for us, who can be against us?

Romans 8:31

Nay, in all these things we are more than conquerors through him that loved us.

For I am persuaded, that neither death, nor life, nor angels, nor principalities, nor powers, nor things present, nor things to come,

Nor height, nor depth, nor any other creature, shall be able to separate us from the love of God, which is in Christ Jesus our Lord.

Romans 8:37-39

Fear thou not; for I am with thee: be not dismayed; for I am thy God: I will strengthen thee; yea, I will help thee; yea, I will uphold thee with the right hand of my righteousness.

Isaiah 41:10

Humble yourselves therefore under the mighty hand of God, that he may exalt you in due time:

Casting all your care upon him; for he careth for you.

1 Peter 5:6,7

Ye are of God, little children, and have overcome them: because greater is he that is in you, than he that is in the world.

1 John 4:4

And they that know thy name will put their trust in thee: for thou, Lord, hast not forsaken them that seek thee.

Psalm 9:10

For the Lord will not cast off his people, neither will he forsake his inheritance.

Psalm 94:14

When my father and my mother forsake me, then the Lord will take me up.

Psalm 27:10

Because he hath set his love upon me, therefore will I deliver him: I will set him on high, because he hath known my name.

He shall call upon me, and I will answer him: I will be with him in trouble; I will deliver him, and honour him.

Psalm 91:14,15

Why art thou cast down, O my soul? and why art thou disquieted within me? hope in God: for I shall yet praise him, who is the health of my countenance, and my God.

Psalm 43:5

Be strong and of a good courage, fear not, nor be afraid of them: for the Lord thy God, he it is that doth go with thee; he will not fail thee, nor forsake thee.

Deuteronomy 31:6

PATIENCE

Better is the end of a thing than the beginning thereof: and the patient in spirit is better than the proud in spirit.

Be not hasty in thy spirit to be angry: for anger resteth in the bosom of fools.

Ecclesiastes 7:8,9

But they that wait upon the Lord shall renew their strength; they shall mount up with wings like eagles; they shall run, and not be weary; and they shall walk, and not faint.

Isaiah 40:31

In your patience possess ye your souls.

Luke 21:19

And not only so, but we glory in tribulations also: knowing that tribulation worketh patience.

And patience, experience; and experience, hope:

And hope maketh not ashamed; because the love of God is shed abroad in our hearts by the Holy Ghost which is given unto us.

Romans 5:3-5

But if we hope for that we see not, then do we with patience wait for it.

Romans 8:25

For whatsoever things were written aforetime were written for our learning, that we through patience and comfort of the scriptures might have hope.

Now the God of patience and consolation grant you to be likeminded one toward another according to Christ Jesus.

Romans 15:4,5

Knowing this, that the trying of your faith worketh patience.

But let patience have her perfect work, that ye may be perfect and entire, wanting nothing.

James 1:3,4

Cast not away therefore your confidence, which hath great recompence of reward.

For ye have need of patience, that, after ye have done the will of God, ye might receive the promise.

For yet a little while, and he that shall come will come, and will not tarry.

Hebrews 10:35-37

That ye be not slothful, but followers of them who through faith and patience inherit the promises.

Hebrews 6:12

And beside this, giving all diligence, add to your faith virtue; and to virtue knowledge.

And to knowledge temperance; and to temperance patience; and to patience godliness.

2 Peter 1:5,6

And let us not be weary in well doing: for in due season we shall reap, if we faint not.

Galatians 6:9

Now we exhort you, brethren, warn them that are unruly, comfort the feebleminded, support the weak, be patient toward all men.

1 Thessalonians 5:14

And so, after he had patiently endured, he obtained the promise.

Hebrews 6:15

Wherefore, my beloved brethren, let every man be swift to hear, slow to speak, slow to wrath.

James 1:19

Be patient therefore, brethren, unto the coming of the Lord. Behold, the husbandman waiteth for the precious fruit of the earth, and hath long patience for it, until he receive the early and latter rain.

Be ye also patient; stablish your hearts: for the coming of the Lord draweth nigh.

James 5:7,8

For what glory is it, if, when ye be buffeted for your faults, ye shall take it patiently? but if, when ye do well, and suffer for it, ye take it patiently, this is acceptable with God.

1 Peter 2:20

But the fruit of the Spirit is love, joy, peace, longsuffering, gentleness, goodness, faith, meekness, temperance: against such there is no law.

Galatians 5:22,23

Wherefore seeing we also are compassed about with so great a cloud of witnesses, let us lay aside every weight, and the sin which doth so easily beset us, and let us run with patience the race that is set before us.

Hebrews 12:1

Rest in the Lord, and wait patiently for him: fret not thyself because of him who prospereth in his way, because of the man who bringeth wicked devices to pass.

Cease from anger, and forsake wrath: fret not thyself in any wise to do evil.

For evildoers shall be cut off: but those that wait upon the Lord, they shall inherit the earth.

Psalm 37:7-9

A wrathful man stirreth up strife: but he that is slow to anger appeaseth strife.

Proverbs 15:18

In your patience possess ye your souls.

Luke 21:19

Charity suffereth long, and is kind; charity envieth not; charity vaunteth not itself, is not puffed up,

Doth not behave itself unseemly, seeketh not her own, is not easily provoked, thinketh no evil.

1 Corinthians 13:4,5

But in all things approving ourselves as the ministers of God, in much patience, in afflictions, in necessities, in distresses.

2 Corinthians 6:4

But thou, O man of God, flee these things; and follow after righteousness, godliness, faith, love, patience, meekness.

1 Timothy 6:11

And the servant of the Lord must not strive; but be gentle unto all men, apt to teach, patient,

In meekness instructing those that oppose themselves; if God peradventure will give them repentance to the acknowledging of the truth.

2 Timothy 2:24,25

Here is the patience of the saints: here are they that keep the commandments of God, and the faith of Jesus.

Revelation 14:12

Forgiving One Another

The discretion of a man deferreth his anger;
and it is his glory to pass over a transgression.

Proverbs 19:11

A friend loveth at all times, and a brother is
born for adversity.

Proverbs 17:17

Put on therefore, as the elect of God, holy and
beloved, bowels of mercies, kindness,
humbleness of mind, meekness, longsuffering.

Forbearing one another, and forgiving one
another, if any man have a quarrel against any:
even as Christ forgave you, so also do ye.

And above all these things put on charity,
which is the bond of perfectness.

Colossians 3:12-14

Hatred stirreth up strifes: but love covereth
all sins.

Proverbs 10:12

Follow peace with all men, and holiness,
without which no man shall see the Lord:

Looking diligently lest any man fail of the grace of God; lest any root of bitterness springing up trouble you, and thereby many be defiled.

Hebrews 12:14,15

Be ye angry, and sin not: let not the sun go down upon your wrath:

Neither give place to the devil.

Ephesians 4:26,27

Blessed are the merciful: for they shall obtain mercy.

Matthew 5:7

For if ye forgive men their trespasses, your heavenly Father will also forgive you:

But if ye forgive not men their trespasses, neither will your Father forgive your trespasses.

Matthew 6:14,15

And when ye stand praying, forgive, if ye have ought against any: that your Father also which is in heaven may forgive you your trespasses.

But if ye do not forgive, neither will your Father which is in heaven forgive your trespasses.

Mark 11:25,26

But love ye your enemies, and do good, and lend, hoping for nothing again; and your reward shall be great, and ye shall be the children of the Highest: for he is kind unto the unthankful and to the evil.

Be ye therefore merciful, as your Father also is merciful.

Judge not, and ye shall not be judged: condemn not, and ye shall not be condemned: forgive, and ye shall be forgiven.

Luke 6:35-37

Take heed to yourselves: If thy brother trespass against thee, rebuke him; and if he repent, forgive him.

And if he trespass against thee seven times in a day, and seven times in a day turn again to thee, saying, I repent; thou shalt forgive him.

Luke 17:3,4

Bless them which persecute you: bless, and curse not.

Romans 12:14

Dearly beloved, avenge not yourselves, but rather give place unto wrath: for it is written, Vengeance is mine; I will repay, saith the Lord.

Romans 12:19

And be ye kind one to another, tenderhearted, forgiving one another, even as God for Christ's sake hath forgiven you.

Ephesians 4:32

Not rendering evil for evil, or railing for railing: but contrariwise blessing; knowing that ye are thereunto called, that ye should inherit a blessing.

1 Peter 3:9

If we confess our sins, he is faithful and just to forgive us our sins, and to cleanse us from all unrighteousness.

1 John 1:9

He that covereth his sins shall not prosper: but whoso confesseth and forsaketh them shall have mercy.

Proverbs 28:13

Charity suffereth long, and is kind; charity envieth not; charity vaunteth not itself, is not puffed up,

Doth not behave itself unseemly, seeketh not her own, is not easily provoked, thinketh no evil.

Rejoiceth not in iniquity, but rejoiceth in the truth.

Beareth all things, believeth all things, hopeth all things, endureth all things.

1 Corinthians 13:4-7

Brethren, if a man be overtaken in a fault, ye which are spiritual, restore such an one in the spirit of meekness; considering thyself, lest thou also be tempted.

Bear ye one another's burdens, and so fulfil the law of Christ.

Galatians 6:1,2

But I say unto you, Love your enemies, bless them that curse you, do good to them that hate you, and pray for them which despitefully use you, and persecute you.

That ye may be the children of your Father which is in heaven: for he maketh his sun to rise on the evil and on the good, and sendeth rain on the just and on the unjust.

Matthew 5:44,45

But love ye your enemies, and do good, and lend, hoping for nothing again; and your reward shall be great, and ye shall be the children of the Highest: for he is kind unto the unthankful and to the evil.

Be ye therefore merciful, as your Father also is merciful.

Judge not, and ye shall not be judged: condemn not, and ye shall not be condemned: forgive, and ye shall be forgiven:

Give, and it shall be given unto you; good measure, pressed down, and shaken together, and running over, shall men give into your bosom. For with the same measure that ye mete withal it shall be measured to you again.

Luke 6:35-38

Finally, brethren, whatsoever things are true, whatsoever things are honest, whatsoever things are just, whatsoever things are pure, whatsoever things are lovely, whatsoever things are of good report; if there be any virtue, and if there be any praise, think on these things.

Philippians 4:8

KNOWING JESUS AS YOUR LORD

Abide in me, and I in you. As the branch cannot bear fruit of itself, except it abide in the vine; no more can ye, except ye abide in me.

I am the vine, ye are the branches: He that abideth in me, and I in him, the same bringeth forth much fruit: for without me ye can do nothing.

If a man abide not in me, he is cast forth as a branch, and is withered; and men gather them, and cast them into the fire, and they are burned.

If ye abide in me, and my words abide in you, ye shall ask what ye will, and it shall be done unto you.

John 15:4-7

Behold, I stand at the door, and knock: if any man hear my voice, and open the door, I will come in to him, and will sup with him, and he with me.

Revelation 3:20

And as Moses lifted up the serpent in the wilderness, even so must the Son of man be lifted up:

That whosoever believeth in him should not perish, but have eternal life.

For God so loved the world, that he gave his only begotten Son, that whosoever believeth in him should not perish, but have everlasting life.

For God sent not his Son into the world to condemn the world; but that the world through him might be saved.

He that believeth on him is not condemned: but he that believeth not is condemned already, because he hath not believed in the name of the only begotten Son of God.

John 3:14-18

Jesus answered and said unto him, Verily, verily, I say unto thee, Except a man be born again, he cannot see the kingdom of God.

John 3:3

And this is the will of him that sent me, that every one which seeth the Son, and believeth on him, may have everlasting life: and I will raise him up at the last day.

John 6:40

Verily, verily, I say unto you, He that believeth on me hath everlasting life.

I am that bread of life.

John 6:47,48

The Father loveth the Son, and hath given all things into his hand.

He that believeth on the Son hath everlasting life: and he that believeth not the Son shall not see life; but the wrath of God abideth on him.

John 3:35,36

For as the Father raiseth up the dead, and quickeneth them; even so the Son quickeneth whom he will.

For the Father judgeth no man, but hath committed all judgment unto the Son:

That all men should honour the Son, even as they honour the Father. He that honoureth not the Son honoureth not the Father which hath sent him.

Verily, verily, I say unto you, He that heareth my word, and believeth on him that sent me, hath everlasting life, and shall not come into condemnation; but is passed from death unto life.

Verily, verily, I say unto you, The hour is coming, and now is, when the dead shall hear the voice of the Son of God: and they that hear shall live.

For as the Father hath life in himself; so hath he given to the Son to have life in himself.

John 5:21-26

I said therefore unto you, that ye shall die in your sins: for if ye believe not that I am he, ye shall die in your sins.

John 8:23,24

The thief cometh not, but for to steal, and to kill, and to destroy: I am come that they might have life, and that they might have it more abundantly.

John 10:10

My sheep hear my voice, and I know them, and they follow me:

And I give unto them eternal life; and they shall never perish, neither shall any man pluck them out of my hand.

My Father, which gave them me, is greater than all; and no man is able to pluck them out of my Father's hand.

I and my Father are one.

John 10:27-30

Jesus said unto her, I am the resurrection, and the life: he that believeth in me, though he were dead, yet shall he live:

And whosoever liveth and believeth in me shall never die. Believest thou this?

John 11:25,26

For there is one God, and one mediator between God and men, the man Christ Jesus.

Who gave himself a ransom for all, to be testified in due time.

1 Timothy 2:5,6

Jesus cried and said, He that believeth on me, believeth not on me, but on him that sent me.

And he that seeth me seeth him that sent me.

I am come a light into the world, that whosoever believeth on me should not abide in darkness.

John 12:44-46

Jesus saith unto him, I am the way, the truth, and the life: no man cometh unto the Father, but by me.

John 14:6

And it shall come to pass, that whosoever shall call on the name of the Lord shall be saved.

Acts 2:21

Repent ye therefore, and be converted, that your sins may be blotted out, when the times of refreshing shall come from the presence of the Lord.

Acts 3:19

Be it known unto you all, and to all the people of Israel, that by the name of Jesus Christ of Nazareth, whom ye crucified, whom God raised from the dead, even by him doth this man stand here before you whole.

This is the stone which was set at nought of you builders, which is become the head of the corner.

Neither is there salvation in any other: for there is none other name under heaven given among men, whereby we must be saved.

Acts 4:10-12

But we believe that through the grace of the Lord Jesus Christ we shall be saved, even as they.

Acts 15:11

That if thou shalt confess with thy mouth the Lord Jesus, and shalt believe in thine heart that God hath raised him from the dead, thou shalt be saved.

For with the heart man believeth unto righteousness; and with the mouth confession is made unto salvation.

Romans 10:9,10

For Christ also hath once suffered for sins, the just for the unjust, that he might bring us to God, being put to death in the flesh, but quickened by the Spirit.

1 Peter 3:18

But as many as received him, to them gave he power to become the sons of God, even to them that believe on his name:

Which were born, not of blood, nor of the will of the flesh, nor of the will of man, but of God.

John 1:12,13

Your relationship with god

And God said, Let us make man in our image, after our likeness: and let them have dominion over the fish of the sea, and over the fowl of the air, and over the cattle, and over all the earth, and over every creeping thing that creepeth upon the earth.

So God created man in his own image, in the image of God created he him; male and female created he them.

Genesis 1:26,27

The Lord is nigh unto all them that call upon him, to all that call upon him in truth.

He will fulfil the desire of them that fear him: he also will hear their cry, and will save them.

Psalm 145:18,19

O taste and see that the Lord is good: blessed is the man that trusteth in him.

Psalm 34:8

The Lord is my strength and song, and he is become my salvation: he is my God, and I will prepare him an habitation; my father's God, and I will exalt him.

Exodus 15:2

The Lord also will be a refuge for the oppressed, a refuge in times of trouble.

And they that know thy name will put their trust in thee: for thou, Lord, hast not forsaken them that seek thee.

Psalm 9:9,10

The Lord is my strength and my shield; my heart trusted in him, and I am helped: therefore my heart greatly rejoiceth; and with my song will I praise him.

Psalm 28:7

God is faithful, by whom ye were called unto the fellowship of his Son Jesus Christ our Lord.

1 Corinthians 1:9

But the salvation of the righteous is of the Lord: he is their strength in the time of trouble.

And the Lord shall help them, and deliver them: he shall deliver them from the wicked, and save them, because they trust in him.

Psalm 37:39,40

For the Lord God is a sun and shield: the Lord will give grace and glory: no good thing will he withhold from them that walk uprightly.

O Lord of hosts, blessed is the man that trusteth in thee.

Psalm 84:11,12

He that dwelleth in the secret place of the most High shall abide under the shadow of the Almighty.

I will say of the Lord, He is my refuge and my fortress: my God; in him will I trust.

Surely he shall deliver thee from the snare of the fowler, and from the noisome pestilence.

He shall cover thee with his feathers, and under his wings shalt thou trust: his truth shall be thy shield and buckler.

Psalm 91:1-4

That which we have seen and heard declare we unto you, that ye also may have fellowship with us: and truly our fellowship is with the Father, and with his Son Jesus Christ.

And these things write we unto you, that your joy may be full.

1 John 1:3,4

But if we walk in the light, as he is in the light, we have fellowship one with another, and the blood of Jesus Christ his Son cleanseth us from all sin.

1 John 1:7

And I will walk among you, and will be your God, and ye shall be my people.

Leviticus 26:12

For ye have not received the spirit of bondage again to fear; but ye have received the Spirit of adoption, whereby we cry, Abba, Father.

Romans 8:15

But to us there is but one God, the Father, of whom are all things, and we in him; and one Lord Jesus Christ, by whom are all things, and we by him.

1 Corinthians 8:6

Blessed be God, even the Father of our Lord Jesus Christ, the Father of mercies, and the God of all comfort.

2 Corinthians 1:3

Paul, an apostle, not of men, neither by man, but by Jesus Christ, and God the Father, who raised him from the dead.

And all the brethren which are with me, unto the churches of Galatia:

Grace be to you and peace from God the Father, and from our Lord Jesus Christ,

Who gave himself for our sins, that he might deliver us from this present evil world, according to the will of God and our Father.

Galatians 1:1-4

But when the fulness of the time was come, God sent forth his Son, made of a woman, made under the law,

To redeem them that were under the law, that we might receive the adoption of sons.

And because ye are sons, God hath sent forth the Spirit of his Son into your hearts, crying, Abba, Father.

Wherefore thou art no more a servant, but a son; and if a son, then an heir of God through Christ.

Galatians 4:4-7

Furthermore we have had fathers of our flesh which corrected us, and we gave them reverence: shall we not much rather be in subjection unto the Father of spirits, and live?

Hebrews 12:9

Every good gift and every perfect gift is from above, and cometh down from the Father of lights, with whom is no variableness, neither shadow of turning.

James 1:17

If ye then, being evil, know how to give good gifts unto your children: how much more shall your heavenly Father give the Holy Spirit to them that ask him?

Luke 11:13

If ye then, being evil, know how to give good gifts unto your children, how much more shall your Father which is in heaven give good things to them that ask him?

Matthew 7:11

Studying God's Word

This book of the law shall not depart out of thy mouth; but thou shalt meditate therein day and night, that thou mayest observe to do according to all that is written therein: for then thou shalt make thy way prosperous, and then thou shalt have good success.

Joshua 1:8

And that from a child thou hast known the holy scriptures, which are able to make thee wise unto salvation through faith which is in Christ Jesus.

All scripture is given by inspiration of God, and is profitable for doctrine, for reproof, for correction, for instruction in righteousness.

2 Timothy 3:15,16

Heaven and earth shall pass away: but my words shall not pass away.

Mark 13:31

But he answered and said, It is written, Man shall not live by bread alone, but by every word that proceedeth out of the mouth of God.

Matthew 4:4

Study to shew thyself approved unto God, a workman that needeth not to be ashamed, rightly dividing the word of truth.

2 Timothy 2:15

But his delight is in the law of the Lord; and in his law doth he meditate day and night.

Psalm 1:2

Thy word is a lamp unto my feet, and a light unto my path.

Psalm 119:105

As newborn babes, desire the sincere milk of the word, that ye may grow thereby.

1 Peter 2:2

Then said Jesus to those Jews which believed on him, If ye continue in my word, then are ye my disciples indeed.

And ye shall know the truth, and the truth shall make you free.

John 8:31,32

So then faith cometh by hearing, and hearing by the word of God.

Romans 10:17

For whatsoever things were written aforetime were written for our learning, that we through patience and comfort of the scriptures might have hope.

Romans 15:4

The grass withereth, the flower fadeth: but the word of our God shall stand for ever.

Isaiah 40:8

My son, forget not my law; but let thine heart keep my commandments:
For length of days, and long life, and peace, shall they add to thee.
Let not mercy and truth forsake thee: bind them about thy neck; write them upon the table of thine heart:
So shalt thou find favour and good understanding in the sight of God and man.

Proverbs 3:1-4

The entrance of thy words giveth light; it giveth understanding unto the simple.

Psalm 119:130

Thy word have I hid in mine heart, that I might not sin against thee.

Psalm 119:11

For the word of God is quick, and powerful, and sharper than any twoedged sword, piercing even to the dividing asunder of soul and spirit, and of the joints and marrow, and is a discerner of the thoughts and intents of the heart.

Hebrews 4:12

For the prophecy came not in old time by the will of man: but holy men of God spake as they were moved by the Holy Ghost.

2 Peter 1:21

Blessed is he that readeth, and they that hear the words of this prophecy, and keep those things which are written therein: for the time is at hand.

Revelation 1:3

Search the scriptures; for in them ye think ye have eternal life: and they are they which testify of me.

John 5:39

But the word is very nigh unto thee, in thy mouth, and in thy heart, that thou mayest do it.

Deuteronomy 30:14

Be ye mindful always of his covenant; the word which he commanded to a thousand generations.

1 Chronicles 16:15

Receive, I pray thee, the law from his mouth, and lay up his words in thine heart.

Job 22:22

Neither have I gone back from the commandment of his lips; I have esteemed the words of his mouth more than my necessary food.

Job 23:12

The law of his God is in his heart; none of his steps shall slide.

Psalm 37:31

When thou goest, it shall lead thee; when thou sleepest, it shall keep thee; and when thou awakest, it shall talk with thee.

For the commandment is a lamp; and the law is light; and reproofs of instruction are the way of life.

Proverbs 6:22,23

Therefore whosoever heareth these sayings of mine, and doeth them, I will liken him unto a wise man, which built his house upon a rock.

Matthew 7:24

Jesus answered and said unto them, Ye do err, not knowing the scriptures, nor the power of God.

Matthew 22:29

And these words, which I command thee this day, shall be in thine heart.

Deuteronomy 6:6

The secret things belong unto the Lord our God: but those things which are revealed belong unto us and to our children for ever, that we may do all the words of this law.

Deuteronomy 29:29

But the word is very nigh unto thee, in thy mouth, and in thy heart, that thou mayest do it.

Deuteronomy 30:14

Wherewithal shall a young man cleanse his way? by taking heed thereto according to thy word.

Psalm 119:9

DEVELOPING YOUR PRAYER LIFE

If my people, which are called by my name, shall humble themselves, and pray, and seek my face, and turn from their wicked ways; then will I hear from heaven, and will forgive their sin, and will heal their land.

2 Chronicles 7:14

The Lord is near unto all those who call upon him, to all who call upon him in truth.

Psalm 145:18

Let us, therefore, come boldly unto the throne of grace, that we may obtain mercy, and find grace to help in time of need.

Hebrews 4:16

Call unto me, and I will answer thee, and shew thee great and mighty things, which thou knowest not.

Jeremiah 33:3

And all things, whatsoever ye shall ask in prayer, believing, ye shall receive.

Matthew 21:22

91

Again I say unto you, That if two of you shall agree on earth as touching any thing that they shall ask, it shall be done for them of my Father which is in heaven.

Matthew 18:19

Continue in prayer, and watch in the same with thanksgiving.

Colossians 4:2

The eyes of the Lord are upon the righteous, and his ears are open unto their cry.

Psalm 34:15

Confess your faults one to another, and pray one for another, that ye may be healed. The effectual fervent prayer of a righteous man availeth much.

Elias was a man subject to like passions as we are, and he prayed earnestly that it might not rain: and it rained not on the earth by the space of three years and six months.

And he prayed again, and the heaven gave rain, and the earth brought forth her fruit.

James 5:16-18

And this is the confidence that we have in him, that, if we ask any thing according to his will, he heareth us:

And if we know that he hear us, whatsoever we ask, we know that we have the petitions that we desired of him.

1 John 5:14,15

Watch ye therefore, and pray always, that ye may be accounted worthy to escape all these things that shall come to pass, and to stand before the Son of man.

Luke 21:36

When thou saidst, Seek ye my face; my heart said unto thee, Thy face, Lord, will I seek.

Psalm 27:8

Ask, and it shall be given you; seek, and ye shall find; knock, and it shall be opened unto you:

For every one that asketh receiveth; and he that seeketh findeth; and to him that knocketh it shall be opened.

Matthew 7:7,8

For verily I say unto you, That whosoever shall say unto this mountain, Be thou removed, and be thou cast into the sea; and shall not doubt in his heart, but shall believe that those things which he saith shall come to pass; he shall have whatsoever he saith.

Therefore I say unto you, What things soever ye desire, when ye pray, believe that ye receive them, and ye shall have them.

And when ye stand praying, forgive, if ye have ought against any: that your Father also which is in heaven may forgive you your trespasses.

Mark 11:23-25

Be careful for nothing; but in every thing by prayer and supplication with thanksgiving let your requests be made known unto God.

Philippians 4:6

If ye abide in me, and my words abide in you, ye shall ask what ye will, and it shall be done unto you.

John 15:7

And whatsoever ye shall ask in my name, that will I do, that the Father may be glorified in the Son.

If ye shall ask any thing in my name, I will do it.

John 14:13,14

And in that day ye shall ask me nothing. Verily, verily, I say unto you, Whatsoever ye shall ask the Father in my name, he will give it you.

Hitherto have ye asked nothing in my name: ask, and ye shall receive, that your joy may be full.

John 16:23,24

But ye, beloved, building up yourselves on your most holy faith, praying in the Holy Spirit,

Jude 20

For the people shall dwell in Zion at Jerusalem: thou shalt weep no more: he will be very gracious unto thee at the voice of thy cry; when he shall hear it, he will answer thee.

Isaiah 30:19

Then shall ye call upon me, and ye shall go and pray unto me, and I will hearken unto you.

Jeremiah 29:12

And it shall come to pass, that before they call, I will answer; and while they are yet speaking, I will hear.

Isaiah 65:24

And when thou prayest, thou shalt not be as the hypocrites are: for they love to pray standing in the synagogues and in the corners of the streets, that they may be seen of men. Verily I say unto you, They have their reward.

But thou, when thou prayest, enter into thy closet, and when thou hast shut thy door, pray to thy Father which is in secret; and thy Father which seeth in secret shall reward thee openly.

But when ye pray, use not vain repetitions, as the heathen do: for they think that they shall be heard for their much speaking.

Be not ye therefore like unto them: for your Father knoweth what things ye have need of, before ye ask him.

After this manner therefore pray ye: Our Father which art in heaven, Hallowed be thy name.

Thy kingdom come. Thy will be done in earth, as it is in heaven.

Give us this day our daily bread.

And forgive us our debts, as we forgive our debtors.

And lead us not into temptation, but deliver us from evil: For thine is the kingdom, and the power, and the glory, for ever. Amen.

Matthew 6:5-13

If ye then, being evil, know how to give good gifts unto your children, how much more shall your Father which is in heaven give good things to them that ask him?

Matthew 7:11

The Lord is far from the wicked: but he heareth the prayer of the righteous.

Proverbs 15:29

Evening, and morning, and at noon, will I pray, and cry aloud: and he shall hear my voice.

Psalm 55:17

The Lord is nigh unto all them that call upon him, to all that call upon him in truth.

He will fulfil the desire of them that fear him: he also will hear their cry, and will save them.

Psalm 145:18,19

And whatsoever we ask, we receive of him, because we keep his commandments, and do those things that are pleasing in his sight.

1 John 3:22

Seek the Lord and his strength, seek his face continually.

1 Chronicles 16:11

Praise and Worship

But the hour cometh, and now is, when the true worshippers shall worship the Father in spirit and in truth: for the Father seeketh such to worship him.

God is a Spirit: and they that worship him must worship him in spirit and in truth.

John 4:23,24

O come, let us worship and bow down: let us kneel before the Lord our maker.

Psalm 95:6

Give unto the Lord the glory due unto his name; worship the Lord in the beauty of holiness.

Psalm 29:2

O Lord, thou art my God; I will exalt thee, I will praise thy name; for thou hast done wonderful things; thy counsels of old are faithfulness and truth.

Isaiah 25:1

I will praise thee; for I am fearfully and wonderfully made: marvellous are thy works; and that my soul knoweth right well.

Psalm 139:14

And my tongue shall speak of thy righteousness and of thy praise all the day long.

Psalm 35:28

And to stand every morning to thank and praise the Lord, and likewise at even.

1 Chronicles 23:30

The Lord is my strength and my shield; my heart trusted in him, and I am helped: therefore my heart greatly rejoiceth; and with my song will I praise him.

Psalm 28:7

I will bless the Lord at all times: his praise shall continually be in my mouth.

Psalm 34:1

He that dwelleth in the secret place of the most High shall abide under the shadow of the Almighty.
I will say of the Lord, He is my refuge and my fortress: my God; in him will I trust.

Psalm 91:1,2

So we thy people and sheep of thy pasture will give thee thanks for ever: we will shew forth thy praise to all generations.

Psalm 79:13

Rejoice in the Lord, O ye righteous: for praise is comely for the upright.

Praise the Lord with harp: sing unto him with the psaltery and an instrument of ten strings.

Sing unto him a new song; play skilfully with a loud noise.

Psalm 33:1-3

Whoso offereth praise glorifieth me: and to him that ordereth his conversation aright will I shew the salvation of God.

Psalm 50:23

O come, let us sing unto the Lord: let us make a joyful noise to the rock of our salvation.

Let us come before his presence with thanksgiving, and make a joyful noise unto him with psalms.

For the Lord is a great God, and a great King above all gods.

Psalm 95:1-3

Then saith Jesus unto him, Get thee hence, Satan: for it is written, Thou shalt worship the Lord thy God, and him only shalt thou serve.

Matthew 4:10

I will praise the Lord according to his righteousness: and will sing praise to the name of the Lord most high.

Psalm 7:17

Sing praises to the Lord, which dwelleth in Zion: declare among the people his doings.

Psalm 9:11

And one of them, when he saw that he was healed, turned back, and with a loud voice glorified God,

And fell down on his face at his feet, giving him thanks: and he was a Samaritan.

Luke 17:15,16

And they worshipped him, and returned to Jerusalem with great joy:

And were continually in the temple, praising and blessing God.

Luke 24:52,53

Now unto him that is able to do exceeding abundantly above all that we ask or think, according to the power that worketh in us,

Unto him be glory in the church by Christ Jesus throughout all ages, world without end.

Ephesians 3:20,21

Speaking to yourselves in psalms and hymns and spiritual songs, singing and making melody in your heart to the Lord.

Ephesians 5:19

Now unto the King eternal, immortal, invisible, the only wise God, be honour and glory for ever and ever.

1 Timothy 1:17

By him therefore let us offer the sacrifice of praise to God continually, that is, the fruit of our lips giving thanks to his name.

Hebrews 13:15

But ye are a chosen generation, a royal priesthood, an holy nation, a peculiar people; that ye should shew forth the praises of him who hath called you out of darkness into his marvellous light.

1 Peter 2:9

For we are the circumcision, which worship God in the spirit, and rejoice in Christ Jesus, and have no confidence in the flesh.

Philippians 3:3

I will therefore that men pray every where, lifting up holy hands, without wrath and doubting.

1 Timothy 2:8

Praying for Your Spouse

For the eyes of the Lord are over the righteous, and his ears are open unto their prayers: but the face of the Lord is against them that do evil.

1 Peter 3:12

That their hearts might be comforted, being knit together in love, and unto all riches of the full assurance of understanding, to the acknowledgement of the mystery of God, and of the Father, and of Christ.

In whom are hid all the treasures of wisdom and knowledge.

Colossians 2:2,3

That the God of our Lord Jesus Christ, the Father of glory, may give unto you the spirit of wisdom and revelation in the knowledge of him:

The eyes of your understanding being enlightened; that ye may know what is the hope of his calling, and what the riches of the glory of his inheritance in the saints,

And what is the exceeding greatness of his power to us-ward who believe, according to the working of his mighty power,

Which he wrought in Christ, when he raised him from the dead, and set him at his own right hand in the heavenly places,

Far above all principality, and power, and might, and dominion, and every name that is named, not only in this world, but also in that which is to come:

And hath put all things under his feet, and gave him to be the head over all things to the church,

Which is his body, the fulness of him that filleth all in all.

Ephesians 1:17-23

Wherefore also we pray always for you, that our God would count you worthy of this calling, and fulfil all the good pleasure of his goodness, and the work of faith with power:

That the name of our Lord Jesus Christ may be glorified in you, and ye in him, according to the grace of our God and the Lord Jesus Christ.

2 Thessalonians 1:11,12

Praying always with all prayer and supplication in the Spirit, and watching thereunto with all perseverance and supplication for all saints.

Ephesians 6:18

For this cause I bow my knees unto the Father of our Lord Jesus Christ,

Of whom the whole family in heaven and earth is named,

That he would grant you, according to the riches of his glory, to be strengthened with might by his Spirit in the inner man.

That Christ may dwell in your hearts by faith; that ye, being rooted and grounded in love,

May be able to comprehend with all saints what is the breadth, and length, and depth, and height;

And to know the love of Christ, which passeth knowledge, that ye might be filled with all the fulness of God.

Now unto him that is able to do exceeding abundantly above all that we ask or think, according to the power that worketh in us,

Unto him be glory in the church by Christ Jesus throughout all ages, world without end. Amen.

Ephesians 3:14-21

And this I pray, that your love may abound yet more and more in knowledge and in all judgment;

That ye may approve things that are excellent; that ye may be sincere and without offence till the day of Christ.

Being filled with the fruits of righteousness, which are by Jesus Christ, unto the glory and praise of God.

Philippians 1:9-11

For this cause we also, since the day we heard it, do not cease to pray for you, and to desire that ye might be filled with the knowledge of his will in all wisdom and spiritual understanding.

That ye might walk worthy of the Lord unto all pleasing, being fruitful in every good work, and increasing in the knowledge of God;

Strengthened with all might, according to his glorious power, unto all patience and longsuffering with joyfulness;

Giving thanks unto the Father, which hath made us meet to be partakers of the inheritance of the saints in light:

Who hath delivered us from the power of darkness, and hath translated us into the kingdom of his dear Son:

In whom we have redemption through his blood, even the forgiveness of sins:

Colossians 1:9-14

I entreated thy favour with my whole heart: be merciful unto me according to thy word.

Psalm 119:58

Likewise the Spirit also helpeth our infirmities: for we know not what we should pray for as we ought: but the Spirit itself maketh intercession for us with groanings which cannot be uttered.

Romans 8:26

For the perfecting of the saints, for the work of the ministry, for the edifying of the body of Christ.

Ephesians 4:12

Wherefore also we pray always for you, that our God would count you worthy of this calling, and fulfil all the good pleasure of his goodness, and the work of faith with power:

That the name of our Lord Jesus Christ may be glorified in you, and ye in him, according to the grace of our God and the Lord Jesus Christ.

2 Thessalonians 1:11,12

Now the God of peace, that brought again from the dead our Lord Jesus, that great shepherd of the sheep, through the blood of the everlasting covenant,

Make you perfect in every good work to do his will, working in you that which is wellpleasing in his sight, through Jesus Christ; to whom be glory for ever and ever. Amen.

Hebrews 13:20,21

Seeking after God

But seek ye first the kingdom of God, and his righteousness; and all these things shall be added unto you.

Matthew 6:33

If ye then be risen with Christ, seek those things which are above, where Christ sitteth on the right hand of God.

Set your affection on things above, not on things on the earth.

For ye are dead, and your life is hid with Christ in God.

When Christ, who is our life, shall appear, then shall ye also appear with him in glory.

Colossians 3:1-4

Draw nigh to God, and he will draw nigh to you. Cleanse your hands, ye sinners; and purify your hearts, ye double minded.

James 4:8

One thing have I desired of the Lord, that will I seek after; that I may dwell in the house of the Lord all the days of my life, to behold the beauty of the Lord, and to inquire in his temple.

Psalm 27:4

When thou saidst, Seek ye my face; my heart said unto thee, Thy face, Lord, will I seek.

Hide not thy face far from me; put not thy servant away in anger: thou hast been my help; leave me not, neither forsake me, O God of my salvation.

Psalm 27:8,9

O fear the Lord, ye his saints: for there is no want to them that fear him.

The young lions do lack, and suffer hunger: but they that seek the Lord shall not want any good thing.

Psalm 34:9,10

Trust in him at all times; ye people, pour out your heart before him: God is a refuge for us.

Psalm 62:8

The humble shall see this, and be glad: and your heart shall live that seek God.

Psalm 69:32

Glory ye in his holy name: let the heart of them rejoice that seek the Lord.

Seek the Lord, and his strength: seek his face evermore.

Psalm 105:3,4

Yea, in the way of thy judgments, O Lord, have we waited for thee; the desire of our soul is to thy name, and to the remembrance of thee.

With my soul have I desired thee in the night; yea, with my spirit within me will I seek thee early: for when thy judgments are in the earth, the inhabitants of the world will learn righteousness.

Isaiah 26:8,9

But if from thence thou shalt seek the Lord thy God, thou shalt find him, if thou seek him with all thy heart and with all thy soul.

Deuteronomy 4:29

Seek the Lord and his strength, seek his face continually.

Remember his marvellous works that he hath done, his wonders, and the judgments of his mouth.

1 Chronicles 16:11,12

And they that know thy name will put their trust in thee: for thou, Lord, hast not forsaken them that seek thee.

Psalm 9:10

When thou saidst, Seek ye my face; my heart said unto thee, Thy face, Lord, will I seek.

Psalm 27:8

O God, thou art my God; early will I seek thee: my soul thirsteth for thee, my flesh longeth for thee in a dry and thirsty land, where no water is.

To see thy power and thy glory, so as I have seen thee in the sanctuary.

Psalm 63:1,2

Let all those that seek thee rejoice and be glad in thee: and let such as love thy salvation say continually, Let God be magnified.

Psalm 70:4

Hearken to me, ye that follow after righteousness, ye that seek the Lord: look unto the rock whence ye are hewn, and to the hole of the pit whence ye are digged.

Isaiah 51:1

Seek ye the Lord while he may be found, call ye upon him while he is near:

Let the wicked forsake his way, and the unrighteous man his thoughts: and let him return unto the Lord, and he will have mercy upon him; and to our God, for he will abundantly pardon.

Isaiah 55:6,7

Seek ye the Lord, all ye meek of the earth, which have wrought his judgment; seek righteousness, seek meekness: it may be ye shall be hid in the day of the Lord's anger.

Zephaniah 2:3

Ask, and it shall be given you; seek, and ye shall find; knock, and it shall be opened unto you.

Matthew 7:7

If ye then be risen with Christ, seek those things which are above, where Christ sitteth on the right hand of God.

Set your affection on things above, not on things on the earth.

For ye are dead, and your life is hid with Christ in God.

Colossians 3:1-3

But without faith it is impossible to please him: for he that cometh to God must believe that he is, and that he is a rewarder of them that diligently seek him.

Hebrews 11:6

For he that will love life, and see good days, let him refrain his tongue from evil, and his lips that they speak no guile:

Let him eschew evil, and do good; let him seek peace, and ensue it.

For the eyes of the Lord are over the righteous, and his ears are open unto their prayers: but the face of the Lord is against them that do evil.

1 Peter 3:10-12

That they should seek the Lord, if haply they might feel after him, and find him, though he be not far from every one of us.

Acts 17:27

111

The Lord is good unto them that wait for him, to the soul that seeketh him.

Lamentations 3:25

For thus saith the Lord unto the house of Israel, Seek ye me, and ye shall live.

Amos 5:4

For I was ashamed to require of the king a band of soldiers and horsemen to help us against the enemy in the way: because we had spoken unto the king, saying, The hand of our God is upon all them for good that seek him; but his power and his wrath is against all them that forsake him.

Ezra 8:22

And they that know thy name will put their trust in thee: for thou, Lord, hast not forsaken them that seek thee.

Psalm 9:10

And ye shall seek me, and find me, when ye shall search for me with all your heart.

Jeremiah 29:13

And thou shalt love the Lord thy God with all thine heart, and with all thy soul, and with all thy might.

Deuteronomy 6:5

Attending Your Local Church

And let us consider one another to provoke unto love and to good works:

Not forsaking the assembling of ourselves together, as the manner of some is; but exhorting one another: and so much the more, as ye see the day approaching.

Hebrews 10:24,25

And if one prevail against him, two shall withstand him; and a threefold cord is not quickly broken.

Ecclesiastes 4:12

Behold, how good and how pleasant it is for brethren to dwell together in unity!

Psalm 133:1

Endeavouring to keep the unity of the Spirit in the bond of peace.

Ephesians 4:3

Till we all come in the unity of the faith, and of the knowledge of the Son of God, unto a perfect man, unto the measure of the stature of the fulness of Christ.

Ephesians 4:13

Ye also, as lively stones, are built up a spiritual house, an holy priesthood, to offer up spiritual sacrifices, acceptable to God by Jesus Christ.

1 Peter 2:5

Then they that gladly received his word were baptized: and the same day there were added unto them about three thousand souls.

And they continued stedfastly in the apostles' doctrine and fellowship, and in breaking of bread, and in prayers.

Acts 2:41,42

And they, continuing daily with one accord in the temple, and breaking bread from house to house, did eat their meat with gladness and singleness of heart,

Praising God, and having favour with all the people. And the Lord added to the church daily such as should be saved.

Acts 2:46,47

For where two or three are gathered together in my name, there am I in the midst of them.

Matthew 18:20

For as we have many members in one body, and all members have not the same office:

So we, being many, are one body in Christ, and every one members one of another.

Romans 12:4,5

For as the body is one, and hath many members, and all the members of that one body, being many, are one body: so also is Christ.

For by one Spirit are we all baptized into one body, whether we be Jews or Gentiles, whether we be bond or free; and have been all made to drink into one Spirit.

For the body is not one member, but many.

1 Corinthians 12:12-14

But now hath God set the members every one of them in the body, as it hath pleased him.

And if they were all one member, where were the body?

But now are they many members, yet but one body.

1 Corinthians 12:18-20

And God hath set some in the church, first apostles, secondarily prophets, thirdly teachers, after that miracles, then gifts of healings, helps, governments, diversities of tongues.

1 Corinthians 12:28

Praise ye the Lord. I will praise the Lord with my whole heart, in the assembly of the upright, and in the congregation.

Psalm 111:1

ROMANCE AND SEX IN MARRIAGE

Drink waters out of thine own cistern, and running waters out of thine own well.

Let thy fountains be dispersed abroad, and rivers of waters in the streets.

Let them be only thine own, and not strangers' with thee.

Let thy fountain be blessed: and rejoice with the wife of thy youth.

Let her be as the loving hind and pleasant roe; let her breasts satisfy thee at all times; and be thou ravished always with her love.

Proverbs 5:15-19

Let him kiss me with the kisses of his mouth: for thy love is better than wine.

Song of Solomon 1:2

His left hand is under my head, and his right hand doth embrace me.

Song of Solomon 2:6

I am my beloved's, and his desire is toward me.

Song of Solomon 7:10

Many waters cannot quench love, neither can the floods drown it: if a man would give all the substance of his house for love, it would utterly be contemned.

Song of Solomon 8:7

Behold, thou art fair, my love; behold, thou art fair; thou hast doves' eyes within thy locks: thy hair is as a flock of goats, that appear from mount Gilead.

Thy teeth are like a flock of sheep that are even shorn, which came up from the washing; whereof every one bear twins, and none is barren among them.

Thy lips are like a thread of scarlet, and thy speech is comely: thy temples are like a piece of a pomegranate within thy locks.

Thy neck is like the tower of David builded for an armoury, whereon there hang a thousand bucklers, all shields of mighty men.

Thy two breasts are like two young roes that are twins, which feed among the lilies.

Until the day break, and the shadows flee away, I will get me to the mountain of myrrh, and to the hill of frankincense.

Thou art all fair, my love; there is no spot in thee.

Song of Solomon 4:1-7

Draw me, we will run after thee: the king hath brought me into his chambers: we will be glad and rejoice in thee, we will remember thy love more than wine: the upright love thee.

Song of Solomon 1:4

I have compared thee, O my love, to a company of horses in Pharaoh's chariots.

Thy cheeks are comely with rows of jewels, thy neck with chains of gold.

We will make thee borders of gold with studs of silver.

While the king sitteth at his table, my spikenard sendeth forth the smell thereof.

A bundle of myrrh is my wellbeloved unto me; he shall lie all night betwixt my breasts.

My beloved is unto me as a cluster of camphire in the vineyards of En-gedi.

Behold, thou art fair, my love; behold, thou art fair; thou hast doves' eyes.

Behold, thou art fair, my beloved, yea, pleasant: also our bed is green.

The beams of our house are cedar, and our rafters of fir.

Song of Solomon 1:9-17

O my dove, that art in the clefts of the rock, in the secret places of the stairs, let me see thy countenance, let me hear thy voice; for sweet is thy voice, and thy countenance is comely.

Song of Solomon 2:14

Thou hast ravished my heart, my sister, my spouse; thou hast ravished my heart with one of thine eyes, with one chain of thy neck.

How fair is thy love, my sister, my spouse! how much better is thy love than wine! and the smell of thine ointments than all spices!

Thy lips, O my spouse, drop as the honeycomb: honey and milk are under thy tongue; and the smell of thy garments is like the smell of Lebanon.

A garden enclosed is my sister, my spouse; a spring shut up, a fountain sealed.

Song of Solomon 4:9-12

My beloved is white and ruddy, the chiefest among ten thousand.

His head is as the most fine gold, his locks are bushy, and black as a raven.

His eyes are as the eyes of doves by the rivers of waters, washed with milk, and fitly set.

His cheeks are as a bed of spices, as sweet flowers: his lips like lilies, dropping sweet smelling myrrh.

His hands are as gold rings set with the beryl: his belly is as bright ivory overlaid with sapphires.

His legs are as pillars of marble, set upon sockets of fine gold: his countenance is as Lebanon, excellent as the cedars.

His mouth is most sweet: yea, he is altogether lovely. This is my beloved, and this is my friend, O daughters of Jerusalem.

Song of Solomon 5:10-16

I am my beloved's, and my beloved is mine: he feedeth among the lilies.

Thou art beautiful, O my love, as Tirzah, comely as Jerusalem, terrible as an army with banners.

Turn away thine eyes from me, for they have overcome me: thy hair is as a flock of goats that appear from Gilead.

Thy teeth are as a flock of sheep which go up from the washing, whereof every one beareth twins, and there is not one barren among them.

Song of Solomon 6:3-6

How beautiful are thy feet with shoes, O prince's daughter! the joints of thy thighs are like jewels, the work of the hands of a cunning workman.

Thy navel is like a round goblet, which wanteth not liquor: thy belly is like an heap of wheat set about with lilies.

Thy two breasts are like two young roes that are twins.

Thy neck is as a tower of ivory; thine eyes like the fishpools in Heshbon, by the gate of Bath-rabbim: thy nose is as the tower of Lebanon which looketh toward Damascus.

Thine head upon thee is like Carmel, and the hair of thine head like purple; the king is held in the galleries.

How fair and how pleasant art thou, O love, for delights!

This thy stature is like to a palm tree, and thy breasts to clusters of grapes.

I said, I will go up to the palm tree, I will take hold of the boughs thereof: now also thy breasts shall be as clusters of the vine, and the smell of thy nose like apples.

And the roof of thy mouth like the best wine for my beloved, that goeth down sweetly, causing the lips of those that are asleep to speak.

Song of Solomon 7:1-9

His left hand should be under my head, and his right hand should embrace me.

Song of Solomon 8:3

Let the husband render unto the wife due benevolence: and likewise also the wife unto the husband.

The wife hath not power of her own body, but the husband: and likewise also the husband hath not power of his own body, but the wife.

Defraud ye not one the other, except it be with consent for a time, that ye may give yourselves to fasting and prayer; and come together again, that Satan tempt you not for your incontinency.

1 Corinthians 7:3-5

Marriage is honourable in all, and the bed undefiled: but whoremongers and adulterers God will judge.

Hebrews 13:4

A bundle of myrrh is my wellbeloved unto me; he shall lie all night betwixt my breasts.

Song of Solomon 1:13

F AITHFULNESS

And he answered and said unto them, Have ye not read, that he which made them at the beginning made them male and female,

And said, For this cause shall a man leave father and mother, and shall cleave to his wife: and they twain shall be one flesh?

Wherefore they are no more twain, but one flesh. What therefore God hath joined together, let not man put asunder.

Matthew 19:4-6

But from the beginning of the creation God made them male and female.

For this cause shall a man leave his father and mother, and cleave to his wife;

And they twain shall be one flesh: so then they are no more twain, but one flesh.

What therefore God hath joined together, let not man put asunder.

Mark 10:6-9

Husbands, love your wives, even as Christ also loved the church, and gave himself for it;

That he might sanctify and cleanse it with the washing of water by the word,

That he might present it to himself a glorious church, not having spot, or wrinkle, or any such thing; but that it should be holy and without blemish.

So ought men to love their wives as their own bodies. He that loveth his wife loveth himself.

For no man ever yet hated his own flesh; but nourisheth and cherisheth it, even as the Lord the church:

For we are members of his body, of his flesh, and of his bones.

For this cause shall a man leave his father and mother, and shall be joined unto his wife, and they two shall be one flesh.

This is a great mystery: but I speak concerning Christ and the church.

Nevertheless let every one of you in particular so love his wife even as himself; and the wife see that she reverence her husband.

Ephesians 5:25-33

Therefore shall a man leave his father and his mother, and shall cleave unto his wife: and they shall be one flesh.

Genesis 2:24

Working as unto the Lord

Let him that stole steal no more: but rather let him labour, working with his hands the thing which is good, that he may have to give to him that needeth.

Ephesians 4:28

Thus saith the Lord, thy Redeemer, the Holy One of Israel; I am the Lord thy God which teacheth thee to profit, which leadeth thee by the way that thou shouldest go.

Isaiah 48:17

Commit thy works unto the Lord, and thy thoughts shall be established.

Proverbs 16:3

Cast not away therefore your confidence, which hath great recompence of reward.

Hebrews 10:35

For God is not unrighteous to forget your work and labour of love, which ye have shewed toward his name, in that ye have ministered to the saints, and do minister.

And we desire that every one of you do shew the same diligence to the full assurance of hope unto the end:

That ye be not slothful, but followers of them who through faith and patience inherit the promises.

Hebrews 6:10-12

Be ye strong therefore, and let not your hands be weak: for your work shall be rewarded.

2 Chronicles 15:7

The hand of the diligent shall bear rule: but the slothful shall be under tribute.

Proverbs 12:24

Seest thou a man diligent in his business? he shall stand before kings; he shall not stand before mean men.

Proverbs 22:29

He that tilleth his land shall be satisfied with bread: but he that followeth vain persons is void of understanding.

Proverbs 12:11

A man shall be satisfied with good by the fruit of his mouth: and the recompence of a man's hands shall be rendered unto him.

Proverbs 12:14

The hand of the diligent shall bear rule: but the slothful shall be under tribute.

Proverbs 12:24

The slothful man roasteth not that which he took in hunting: but the substance of a diligent man is precious.

Proverbs 12:27

Wealth gotten by vanity shall be diminished: but he that gathereth by labour shall increase.

Proverbs 13:11

Poverty and shame shall be to him that refuseth instruction: but he that regardeth reproof shall be honoured.

Proverbs 13:18

The desire of the righteous is only good: but the expectation of the wicked is wrath.

Proverbs 11:23

The way of the slothful man is as an hedge of thorns: but the way of the righteous is made plain.

Proverbs 15:19

A just weight and balance are the Lord's: all the weights of the bag are his work.

Proverbs 16:11

Slothfulness casteth into a deep sleep; and an idle soul shall suffer hunger.

Proverbs 19:15

Love not sleep, lest thou come to poverty; open thine eyes, and thou shalt be satisfied with bread.

Proverbs 20:13

He that loveth pleasure shall be a poor man: he that loveth wine and oil shall not be rich.

Proverbs 21:17

Be not among winebibbers; among riotous eaters of flesh:

For the drunkard and the glutton shall come to poverty: and drowsiness shall clothe a man with rags.

Proverbs 23:20,21

Be kindly affectioned one to another with brotherly love; in honour preferring one another.

Not slothful in business; fervent in spirit; serving the Lord.

Romans 12:10,11

He that diligently seeketh good procureth favour: but he that seeketh mischief, it shall come unto him.

Proverbs 11:27

But seek ye first the kingdom of God, and his righteousness; and all these things shall be added unto you.

Matthew 6:33

Now the days of David drew nigh that he should die; and he charged Solomon his son, saying,

I go the way of all the earth: be thou strong therefore, and shew thyself a man.

And keep the charge of the Lord thy God, to walk in his ways, to keep his statutes, and his commandments, and his judgments, and his testimonies, as it is written in the law of Moses, that thou mayest prosper in all that thou doest, and whithersoever thou turnest thyself.

1 Kings 2:1-3

Masters, give unto your servants that which is just and equal; knowing that ye also have a Master in heaven.

Colossians 4:1

And indeed ye do it toward all the brethren which are in all Macedonia: but we beseech you, brethren, that ye increase more and more.

And that ye study to be quiet, and to do your own business, and to work with your own hands, as we commanded you.

That ye may walk honestly toward them that are without, and that ye may have lack of nothing.

1 Thessalonians 4:10-12

Servants, obey in all things your masters according to the flesh; not with eyeservice, as menpleasers; but in singleness of heart, fearing God.

Colossians 3:22

GIVING AND RECEIVING

But this I say, He which soweth sparingly shall reap also sparingly; and he which soweth bountifully shall reap also bountifully.

Every man according as he purposeth in his heart, so let him give; not grudgingly, or of necessity: for God loveth a cheerful giver.

And God is able to make all grace abound toward you; that ye, always having all sufficiency in all things, may abound to every good work:

(As it is written, He hath dispersed abroad; he hath given to the poor: his righteousness remaineth for ever.

Now he that ministereth seed to the sower both minister bread for your food, and multiply your seed sown, and increase the fruits of your righteousness.)

2 Corinthians 9:6-10

Give, and it shall be given unto you; good measure, pressed down, and shaken together, and running over, shall men give into your bosom. For with the same measure that ye mete withal it shall be measured to you again.

Luke 6:38

130

Be not deceived; God is not mocked: for whatsoever a man soweth, that shall he also reap.

Galatians 6:7

I have been young, and now am old; yet have I not seen the righteous forsaken, nor his seed begging bread.

He is ever merciful, and lendeth; and his seed is blessed.

Psalm 37:25,26

Bring ye all the tithes into the storehouse, that there may be meat in mine house, and prove me now herewith, saith the Lord of hosts, if I will not open you the windows of heaven, and pour you out a blessing, that there shall not be room enough to receive it.

And I will rebuke the devourer for your sakes, and he shall not destroy the fruits of your ground; neither shall your vine cast her fruit before the time in the field, saith the Lord of hosts.

And all nations shall call you blessed: for ye shall be a delightsome land, saith the Lord of hosts.

Malachi 3:10-12

Honour the Lord with thy substance, and with the firstfruits of all thine increase:

So shall thy barns be filled with plenty, and thy presses shall burst out with new wine.

Proverbs 3:9,10

He that hath pity upon the poor lendeth unto the Lord; and that which he hath given will he pay him again.

Proverbs 19:17

He that hath a bountiful eye shall be blessed; for he giveth of his bread to the poor.

Proverbs 22:9

But whoso hath this world's good, and seeth his brother have need, and shutteth up his bowels of compassion from him, how dwelleth the love of God in him?

My little children, let us not love in word, neither in tongue; but in deed and in truth.

1 John 3:17,18

Withhold not good from them to whom it is due, when it is in the power of thine hand to do it.

Proverbs 3:27

There is that scattereth, and yet increaseth; and there is that withholdeth more than is meet, but it tendeth to poverty.

The liberal soul shall be made fat: and he that watereth shall be watered also himself.

He that withholdeth corn, the people shall curse him: but blessing shall be upon the head of him that selleth it.

Proverbs 11:24-26

He coveteth greedily all the day long: but the righteous giveth and spareth not.

Proverbs 21:26

And the King shall answer and say unto them, Verily I say unto you, Inasmuch as ye have done it unto one of the least of these my brethren, ye have done it unto me.

Matthew 25:40

When thou vowest a vow unto God, defer not to pay it; for he hath no pleasure in fools: pay that which thou hast vowed.

Better is it that thou shouldest not vow, than that thou shouldest vow and not pay.

Ecclesiastes 5:4,5

Will a man rob God? Yet ye have robbed me. But ye say, Wherein have we robbed thee? In tithes and offerings.

Malachi 3:8

Upon the first day of the week let every one of you lay by him in store, as God hath prospered him, that there be no gatherings when I come.

1 Corinthians 16:2

Heal the sick, cleanse the lepers, raise the dead, cast out devils: freely ye have received, freely give.

Matthew 10:8

A good man leaveth an inheritance to his children's children: and the wealth of the sinner is laid up for the just.

Proverbs 13:22

Making career decisions

And the Lord shall guide thee continually, and satisfy thy soul in drought, and make fat thy bones: and thou shalt be like a watered garden, and like a spring of water, whose waters fail not.

Isaiah 58:11

Trust in the Lord with all thine heart; and lean not unto thine own understanding.

In all thy ways acknowledge him, and he shall direct thy paths.

Proverbs 3:5,6

Thus saith the Lord, thy Redeemer, the Holy One of Israel; I am the Lord thy God which teacheth thee to profit, which leadeth thee by the way that thou shouldest go.

Isaiah 48:17

I will instruct thee and teach thee in the way which thou shalt go: I will guide thee with mine eye.

Psalm 32:8

And I will bring the blind by a way that they knew not; I will lead them in paths that they have not known: I will make darkness light before them, and crooked things straight. These things will I do unto them, and not forsake them.

Isaiah 42:16

And thine ears shall hear a word behind thee, saying, This is the way, walk ye in it, when ye turn to the right hand, and when ye turn to the left.

Isaiah 30:21

Trust in the Lord, and do good; so shalt thou dwell in the land, and verily thou shalt be fed.

Delight thyself also in the Lord; and he shall give thee the desires of thine heart.

Commit thy way unto the Lord; trust also in him; and he shall bring it to pass.

Psalm 37:3-5

Being confident of this very thing, that he which hath begun a good work in you will perform it until the day of Jesus Christ:

Philippians 1:6

Be strong and of a good courage, fear not, nor be afraid of them: for the Lord thy God, he it is that doth go with thee; he will not fail thee, nor forsake thee.

And Moses called unto Joshua, and said unto him in the sight of all Israel, Be strong and of a good courage: for thou must go with this people unto the land which the Lord hath sworn unto their fathers to give them; and thou shalt cause them to inherit it.

And the Lord, he it is that doth go before thee; he will be with thee, he will not fail thee, neither forsake thee: fear not, neither be dismayed.

Deuteronomy 31:6-8

But there is a spirit in man: and the inspiration of the Almighty giveth them understanding.

Job 32:8

I have set the Lord always before me: because he is at my right hand, I shall not be moved.

Psalm 16:8

If any of you lack wisdom, let him ask of God, that giveth to all men liberally, and upbraideth not; and it shall be given him.

James 1:5

The thoughts of the diligent tend only to plenteousness; but of every one that is hasty only to want.

Proverbs 21:5

If any of you lack wisdom, let him ask of God, that giveth to all men liberally, and upbraideth not; and it shall be given him.

But let him ask in faith, nothing wavering, For he that wavereth is like a wave of the sea driven with the wind and tossed.

For let not that man think that he shall receive any thing of the Lord.

A double minded man is unstable in all his ways.

James 1:5-8

A good man sheweth favour, and lendeth: he will guide his affairs with discretion.

Psalm 112:5

It is better to trust in the Lord than to put confidence in man.

It is better to trust in the Lord than to put confidence in princes.

Psalm 118:8,9

Cast thy burden upon the Lord, and he shall sustain thee: he shall never suffer the righteous to be moved.

Psalm 55:22

The Lord will perfect that which concerneth me: thy mercy, O Lord, endureth for ever: forsake not the works of thine own hands.

Psalm 138:8

Commit thy works unto the Lord, and thy thoughts shall be established.

Proverbs 16:3

The entrance of thy words giveth light; it giveth understanding unto the simple.

Psalm 119:130

For the Lord giveth wisdom: out of his mouth cometh knowledge and understanding.

Proverbs 2:6

That the God of our Lord Jesus Christ, the Father of glory, may give unto you the spirit of wisdom and revelation in the knowledge of him:

The eyes of your understanding being enlightened; that ye may know what is the hope of his calling, and what the riches of the glory of his inheritance in the saints.

Ephesians 1:18

This book of the law shall not depart out of thy mouth; but thou shalt meditate therein day and night, that thou mayest observe to do according to all that is written therein: for then thou shalt make thy way prosperous, and then thou shalt have good success.

Joshua 1:8

TRUSTING GOD FOR FINANCES

Delight thyself also in the Lord; and he shall give thee the desires of thine heart.

Psalm 37:4

For the Lord God is a sun and shield: the Lord will give grace and glory: no good thing will he withhold from them that walk uprightly.

Psalm 84:11

Some trust in chariots, and some in horses: but we will remember the name of the Lord our God.

Psalm 20:7

Blessed be the Lord, who daily loadeth us with benefits, even the God of our salvation.

Psalm 68:19

But my God shall supply all your need according to his riches in glory by Christ Jesus.

Philippians 4:19

For ye know the grace of our Lord Jesus Christ, that, though he was rich, yet for your sakes he became poor, that ye through his poverty might be rich.

2 Corinthians 8:9

Jesus said unto him, If thou canst believe, all things are possible to him that believeth.

Mark 9:23

The Lord will not suffer the soul of the righteous to famish: but he casteth away the substance of the wicked.

Proverbs 10:3

Give, and it shall be given unto you; good measure, pressed down, and shaken together, and running over, shall men give into your bosom. For with the same measure that ye mete withal it shall be measured to you again.

Luke 6:38

Thus saith the Lord, thy Redeemer, the Holy One of Israel; I am the Lord thy God which teacheth thee to profit, which leadeth thee by the way that thou shouldest go.

Isaiah 48:17

If ye abide in me, and my words abide in you, ye shall ask what ye will, and it shall be done unto you.

John 15:7

Charge them that are rich in this world, that they be not highminded, nor trust in uncertain riches, but in the living God, who giveth us richly all things to enjoy;

That they do good, that they be rich in good works, ready to distribute, willing to communicate;

Laying up in store for themselves a good foundation against the time to come, that they may lay hold on eternal life.

1 Timothy 6:17-19

Beloved, I wish above all things that thou mayest prosper and be in health, even as thy soul prospereth.

3 John 2

In the house of the righteous is much treasure: but in the revenues of the wicked is trouble.

Proverbs 15:6

By humility and the fear of the Lord are riches, and honour, and life.

Proverbs 22:4

Therefore I say unto you, Take no thought for your life, what ye shall eat, or what ye shall drink; nor yet for your body, what ye shall put on. Is not the life more than meat, and the body than raiment?

Behold the fowls of the air: for they sow not, neither do they reap, nor gather into barns; yet your heavenly Father feedeth them. Are ye not much better than they?

Which of you by taking thought can add one cubit unto his stature?

And why take ye thought for raiment? Consider the lilies of the field, how they grow; they toil not, neither do they spin:

And yet I say unto you, That even Solomon in all his glory was not arrayed like one of these.

Wherefore, if God so clothe the grass of the field, which to day is, and to morrow is cast into the oven, shall he not much more clothe you, O ye of little faith?

Therefore take no thought, saying, What shall we eat? or, What shall we drink? or, Wherewithal shall we be clothed?

(For after all these things do the Gentiles seek:) for your heavenly Father knoweth that ye have need of all these things.

But seek ye first the kingdom of God, and his righteousness; and all these things shall be added unto you.

Take therefore no thought for the morrow: for the morrow shall take thought for the things of itself. Sufficient unto the day is the evil thereof.

Matthew 6:25-34

I have been young, and now am old; yet have I not seen the righteous forsaken, nor his seed begging bread.

He is ever merciful, and lendeth; and his seed is blessed.

Psalm 37:25,26

Blessed be the Lord, who daily loadeth us with benefits, even the God of our salvation.

Psalm 68:19

Trust in the Lord with all thine heart; and lean not unto thine own understanding.

In all thy ways acknowledge him, and he shall direct thy paths.

Proverbs 3:5,6

Cast thy burden upon the Lord, and he shall sustain thee: he shall never suffer the righteous to be moved.

Psalm 55:22

If ye abide in me, and my words abide in you, ye shall ask what ye will, and it shall be done unto you.

John 15:7

Trust ye in the Lord for ever: for in the Lord Jehovah is everlasting strength.

Isaiah 26:4

Blessed is that man that maketh the Lord his trust, and respecteth not the proud, nor such as turn aside to lies.

Psalm 40:4

Trust in the Lord, and do good; so shalt thou dwell in the land, and verily thou shalt be fed.

Delight thyself also in the Lord; and he shall give thee the desires of thine heart.

Commit thy way unto the Lord; trust also in him; and he shall bring it to pass.

Psalm 37:3-5

And he sought God in the days of Zechariah, who had understanding in the visions of God: and as long as he sought the Lord, God made him to prosper.

2 Chronicles 26:5

Blessed is the man that walketh not in the counsel of the ungodly, nor standeth in the way of sinners, nor sitteth in the seat of the scornful.

But his delight is in the law of the Lord; and in his law doth he meditate day and night.

And he shall be like a tree planted by the rivers of water, that bringeth forth his fruit in his season; his leaf also shall not wither; and whatsoever he doeth shall prosper.

Psalm 1:1-3

Be strong and of a good courage: for unto this people shalt thou divide for an inheritance the land, which I sware unto their fathers to give them.

Joshua 1:6

And it shall come to pass, if thou shalt hearken diligently unto the voice of the Lord thy God, to observe and to do all his commandments which I command thee this day, that the Lord thy God will set thee on high above all nations of the earth:

Deuteronomy 28:1

DEALING WITH WORRY

Be careful for nothing; but in every thing by prayer and supplication with thanksgiving let your requests be made known unto God.

And the peace of God, which passeth all understanding, shall keep your hearts and minds through Christ Jesus.

Philippians 4:6,7

Come unto me, all ye that labour and are heavy laden, and I will give you rest.

Take my yoke upon you, and learn of me; for I am meek and lowly in heart: and ye shall find rest unto your souls.

For my yoke is easy, and my burden is light.
Matthew 11:28-30

Therefore I say unto you, Take no thought for your life, what ye shall eat, or what ye shall drink; nor yet for your body, what ye shall put on. Is not the life more than meat, and the body than raiment?

Behold the fowls of the air: for they sow not, neither do they reap, nor gather into barns; yet your heavenly Father feedeth them. Are ye not much better than they?

Which of you by taking thought can add one cubit unto his stature?

And why take ye thought for raiment? Consider the lilies of the field, how they grow; they toil not, neither do they spin:

And yet I say unto you, That even Solomon in all his glory was not arrayed like one of these.

Wherefore, if God so clothe the grass of the field, which to day is, and to morrow is cast into the oven, shall he not much more clothe you, O ye of little faith?

Therefore take no thought, saying, What shall we eat? or, What shall we drink? or, Wherewithal shall we be clothed?

(For after all these things do the Gentiles seek:) for your heavenly Father knoweth that ye have need of all these things.

But seek ye first the kingdom of God, and his righteousness; and all these things shall be added unto you.

Take therefore no thought for the morrow: for the morrow shall take thought for the things of itself. Sufficient unto the day is the evil thereof.

Matthew 6:25-34

Cast thy burden upon the Lord, and he shall sustain thee: he shall never suffer the righteous to be moved.

Psalm 55:22

But the Comforter, which is the Holy Ghost, whom the Father will send in my name, he shall teach you all things, and bring all things to your remembrance, whatsoever I have said unto you.

Peace I leave with you, my peace I give unto you: not as the world giveth, give I unto you. Let not your heart be troubled, neither let it be afraid.

John 14:26,27

Cast not away therefore your confidence, which hath great recompence of reward.

Hebrews 10:35

Humble yourselves therefore under the mighty hand of God, that he may exalt you in due time:

Casting all your care upon him; for he careth for you.

1 Peter 5:6,7

Yea, though I walk through the valley of the shadow of death, I will fear no evil: for thou art with me; thy rod and thy staff they comfort me.

Psalm 23:4

Though I walk in the midst of trouble, thou wilt revive me: thou shalt stretch forth thine hand against the wrath of mine enemies, and thy right hand shall save me.

The Lord will perfect that which concerneth me: thy mercy, O Lord, endureth for ever: forsake not the works of thine own hands.

Psalm 138:7,8

Be strong and of a good courage, fear not, nor be afraid of them: for the Lord thy God, he it is that doth go with thee; he will not fail thee, nor forsake thee.

Deuteronomy 31:6

Thou wilt keep him in perfect peace, whose mind is stayed on thee: because he trusteth in thee.

Isaiah 26:3

Trust in the Lord with all thine heart; and lean not unto thine own understanding.

In all thy ways acknowledge him, and he shall direct thy paths.

Proverbs 3:5,6

The God of my rock; in him will I trust: he is my shield, and the horn of my salvation, my high tower, and my refuge, my saviour; thou savest me from violence.

2 Samuel 22:3

Let us therefore come boldly unto the throne of grace, that we may obtain mercy, and find grace to help in time of need.

Hebrews 4:16

And God is able to make all grace abound toward you; that ye, always having all sufficiency in all things, may abound to every good work.

2 Corinthians 9:8

If they obey and serve him, they shall spend their days in prosperity, and their years in pleasures.

Job 36:11

This book of the law shall not depart out of thy mouth; but thou shalt meditate therein day and night, that thou mayest observe to do according to all that is written therein: for then thou shalt make thy way prosperous, and then thou shalt have good success.

Joshua 1:8

For I the Lord thy God will hold thy right hand, saying unto thee, Fear not; I will help thee.

Isaiah 41:13

The young lions do lack, and suffer hunger: but they that seek the Lord shall not want any good thing.

Psalm 34:10

The Lord is my shepherd; I shall not want.

Psalm 23:1

Let not your heart be troubled: ye believe in God, believe also in me.

John 14:1

DEALING WITH GREED

The thoughts of the diligent tend only to plenteousness; but of every one that is hasty only to want.

Proverbs 21:5

He that trusteth in his riches shall fall: but the righteous shall flourish as a branch.

Proverbs 11:28

Better is little with the fear of the Lord than great treasure and trouble therewith.
Better is a dinner of herbs where love is, than a stalled ox and hatred therewith.

Proverbs 15:16,17

He that is greedy of gain troubleth his own house; but he that hateth gifts shall live.

Proverbs 15:27

The getting of treasures by a lying tongue is a vanity tossed to and fro of them that seek death.

Proverbs 21:6

The desire of the slothful killeth him; for his hands refuse to labour.

He coveteth greedily all the day long: but the righteous giveth and spareth not.

Proverbs 21:25,26

He that oppresseth the poor to increase his riches, and he that giveth to the rich, shall surely come to want.

Proverbs 22:16

Give me now wisdom and knowledge, that I may go out and come in before this people: for who can judge this thy people, that is so great?

And God said to Solomon, Because this was in thine heart, and thou hast not asked riches, wealth, or honour, nor the life of thine enemies, neither yet hast asked long life; but hast asked wisdom and knowledge for thyself, that thou mayest judge my people, over whom I have made thee king:

Wisdom and knowledge is granted unto thee; and I will give thee riches, and wealth, and honour, such as none of the kings have had that have been before thee, neither shall there any after thee have the like.

2 Chronicles 1:10-12

But seek ye first the kingdom of God, and his righteousness; and all these things shall be added unto you.

Matthew 6:33

Lay not up for yourselves treasures upon earth, where moth and rust doth corrupt, and where thieves break through and steal:

But lay up for yourselves treasures in heaven, where neither moth nor rust doth corrupt, and where thieves do not break through nor steal:

For where your treasure is, there will your heart be also.

Matthew 6:19-21

But godliness with contentment is great gain.

For we brought nothing into this world, and it is certain we can carry nothing out.

And having food and raiment let us be therewith content.

But they that will be rich fall into temptation and a snare, and into many foolish and hurtful lusts, which drown men in destruction and perdition.

For the love of money is the root of all evil: which while some coveted after, they have erred from the faith, and pierced themselves through with many sorrows.

But thou, O man of God, flee these things, and follow after righteousness, godliness, faith, love, patience, meekness.

1 Timothy 6:6-11

Charge them that are rich in this world, that they be not highminded, nor trust in uncertain riches, but in the living God, who giveth us richly all things to enjoy.

That they do good, that they be rich in good works, ready to distribute, willing to communicate.

Laying up in store for themselves a good foundation against the time to come, that they may lay hold on eternal life.

1 Timothy 6:17-19

Thou shalt not covet thy neighbour's house, thou shalt not covet thy neighbour's wife, nor his manservant, nor his maidservant, nor his ox, nor his ass, nor any thing that is thy neighbour's.

Exodus 20:17

Incline my heart unto thy testimonies, and not to covetousness.

Psalm 119:36

There is that scattereth, and yet increaseth; and there is that withholdeth more than is meet, but it tendeth to poverty.

Proverbs 11:24

Labour not to be rich: cease from thine own wisdom.

Wilt thou set thine eyes upon that which is not? for riches certainly make themselves wings; they fly away as an eagle toward heaven.

Proverbs 23:4,5

Love not the world, neither the things that are in the world. If any man love the world, the love of the Father is not in him.

1 John 2:15

Feed the flock of God which is among you, taking the oversight thereof, not by constraint, but willingly; not for filthy lucre, but of a ready mind.

1 Peter 5:2

Set your affection on things above, not on things on the earth.

For ye are dead, and your life is hid with Christ in God.

When Christ, who is our life, shall appear, then shall ye also appear with him in glory.

Mortify therefore your members which are upon the earth; fornication, uncleanness, inordinate affection, evil concupiscence, and covetousness, which is idolatry:

For which things' sake the wrath of God cometh on the children of disobedience:

Colossians 3:2-6

Let your conversation be without covetousness; and be content with such things as ye have: for he hath said, I will never leave thee, nor forsake thee.

Hebrews 13:5

But whoso hath this world's good, and seeth his brother have need, and shutteth up his bowels of compassion from him, how dwelleth the love of God in him?

1 John 3:17

STEWARDSHIP

A good man sheweth favour, and lendeth: he will guide his affairs with discretion.

Psalm 112:5

Honour the Lord with thy substance, and with the firstfruits of all thine increase:

So shall thy barns be filled with plenty, and thy presses shall burst out with new wine.

Proverbs 3:9,10

He layeth up sound wisdom for the righteous: he is a buckler to them that walk uprightly.

Proverbs 2:7

There is that scattereth, and yet increaseth; and there is that withholdeth more than is meet, but it tendeth to poverty.

The liberal soul shall be made fat: and he that watereth shall be watered also himself.

He that withholdeth corn, the people shall curse him: but blessing shall be upon the head of him that selleth it.

He that diligently seeketh good procureth favour: but he that seeketh mischief, it shall come unto him.

He that trusteth in his riches shall fall: but the righteous shall flourish as a branch.

Proverbs 11:24-28

Will a man rob God? Yet ye have robbed me. But ye say, Wherein have we robbed thee? In tithes and offerings.

Ye are cursed with a curse: for ye have robbed me, even this whole nation.

Bring ye all the tithes into the storehouse, that there may be meat in mine house, and prove me now herewith, saith the Lord of hosts, if I will not open you the windows of heaven, and pour you out a blessing, that there shall not be room enough to receive it.

And I will rebuke the devourer for your sakes, and he shall not destroy the fruits of your ground; neither shall your vine cast her fruit before the time in the field, saith the Lord of hosts.

And all nations shall call you blessed: for ye shall be a delightsome land, saith the Lord of hosts.

Malachi 3:8-12

But this I say, He which soweth sparingly shall reap also sparingly; and he which soweth bountifully shall reap also bountifully.

Every man according as he purposeth in his heart, so let him give; not grudgingly, or of necessity: for God loveth a cheerful giver.

And God is able to make all grace abound toward you; that ye, always having all sufficiency in all things, may abound to every good work.

2 Corinthians 9:6-8

But lay up for yourselves treasures in heaven, where neither moth nor rust doth corrupt, and where thieves do not break through nor steal:

For where your treasure is, there will your heart be also.

Matthew 6:20,21

Wherefore, if God so clothe the grass of the field, which to day is, and to morrow is cast into the oven, shall he not much more clothe you, O ye of little faith?

Matthew 6:30

And all these blessings shall come on thee, and overtake thee, if thou shalt hearken unto the voice of the Lord thy God.

Blessed shalt thou be in the city, and blessed shalt thou be in the field.

Blessed shall be the fruit of thy body, and the fruit of thy ground, and the fruit of thy cattle, the increase of thy kine, and the flocks of thy sheep.

Blessed shall be thy basket and thy store.

Blessed shalt thou be when thou comest in, and blessed shalt thou be when thou goest out.

The Lord shall cause thine enemies that rise up against thee to be smitten before thy face: they shall come out against thee one way, and flee before thee seven ways.

The Lord shall command the blessing upon thee in thy storehouses, and in all that thou settest thine hand unto; and he shall bless thee in the land which the Lord thy God giveth thee.

The Lord shall establish thee an holy people unto himself, as he hath sworn unto thee, if thou shalt keep the commandments of the Lord thy God, and walk in his ways.

And all people of the earth shall see that thou art called by the name of the Lord; and they shall be afraid of thee.

And the Lord shall make thee plenteous in goods, in the fruit of thy body, and in the fruit of thy cattle, and in the fruit of thy ground, in the land which the Lord sware unto thy fathers to give thee.

The Lord shall open unto thee his good treasure, the heaven to give the rain unto thy land in his season, and to bless all the work of thine hand: and thou shalt lend unto many nations, and thou shalt not borrow.

Deuteronomy 28:2-12

Keep therefore the words of this covenant, and do them, that ye may prosper in all that ye do.

Deuteronomy 29:9

Upon the first day of the week let every one of you lay by him in store, as God hath prospered him, that there be no gatherings when I come.

1 Corinthians 16:2

INVESTING

Thus saith the Lord, thy Redeemer, the Holy One of Israel; I am the Lord thy God which teacheth thee to profit, which leadeth thee by the way that thou shouldest go.

Isaiah 48:17

Bring ye all the tithes into the storehouse, that there may be meat in mine house, and prove me now herewith, saith the Lord of hosts, if I will not open you the windows of heaven, and pour you out a blessing, that there shall not be room enough to receive it.

And I will rebuke the devourer for your sakes, and he shall not destroy the fruits of your ground; neither shall your vine cast her fruit before the time in the field, saith the Lord of hosts.

And all nations shall call you blessed: for ye shall be a delightsome land, saith the Lord of hosts.

Malachi 3:10-12

I will instruct thee and teach thee in the way which thou shalt go: I will guide thee with mine eye.

Psalm 32:8

For which of you, intending to build a tower, sitteth not down first, and counteth the cost, whether he have sufficient to finish it?

Lest haply, after he hath laid the foundation, and is not able to finish it, all that behold it begin to mock him,

Saying, This man began to build, and was not able to finish.

Luke 14:28-30

This book of the law shall not depart out of thy mouth; but thou shalt meditate therein day and night, that thou mayest observe to do according to all that is written therein: for then thou shalt make thy way prosperous, and then thou shalt have good success.

Joshua 1:8

Commit thy works unto the Lord, and thy thoughts shall be established.

Proverbs 16:3

And thine ears shall hear a word behind thee, saying, This is the way, walk ye in it, when ye turn to the right hand, and when ye turn to the left.

Isaiah 30:21

A good man sheweth favour, and lendeth: he will guide his affairs with discretion.

Psalm 112:5

Counsel is mine, and sound wisdom: I am understanding; I have strength.

By me kings reign, and princes decree justice.

By me princes rule, and nobles, even all the judges of the earth.

I love them that love me; and those that seek me early shall find me.

Riches and honour are with me; yea, durable riches and righteousness.

My fruit is better than gold, yea, than fine gold; and my revenue than choice silver.

I lead in the way of righteousness, in the midst of the paths of judgment:

That I may cause those that love me to inherit substance; and I will fill their treasures.

Proverbs 8:14-21

The integrity of the upright shall guide them: but the perverseness of transgressors shall destroy them.

Riches profit not in the day of wrath: but righteousness delivereth from death.

Proverbs 11:3,4

The thoughts of the diligent tend only to plenteousness; but of every one that is hasty only to want.

Proverbs 21:5

By humility and the fear of the Lord are riches, and honour, and life.

Thorns and snares are in the way of the froward: he that doth keep his soul shall be far from them.

Proverbs 22:4,5

Labour not to be rich: cease from thine own wisdom.

Wilt thou set thine eyes upon that which is not? for riches certainly make themselves wings; they fly away as an eagle toward heaven.

Proverbs 23:4,5

But thou shalt remember the Lord thy God: for it is he that giveth thee power to get wealth, that he may establish his covenant which he sware unto thy fathers, as it is this day.

Deuteronomy 8:18

If ye be willing and obedient, ye shall eat the good of the land.

Isaiah 1:19

And he sought God in the days of Zechariah, who had understanding in the visions of God: and as long as he sought the Lord, God made him to prosper.

2 Chronicles 26:5

Blessed is the man that walketh not in the counsel of the ungodly, nor standeth in the way of sinners, nor sitteth in the seat of the scornful.

But his delight is in the law of the Lord; and in his law doth he meditate day and night.

And he shall be like a tree planted by the rivers of water, that bringeth forth his fruit in his season; his leaf also shall not wither; and whatsoever he doeth shall prosper.

Psalm 1:1-3

Keep therefore the words of this covenant, and do them, that ye may prosper in all that ye do.

Deuteronomy 29:9

If they obey and serve him, they shall spend their days in prosperity, and their years in pleasures.

Job 36:11

Beloved, I wish above all things that thou mayest prosper and be in health, even as thy soul prospereth.

3 John 2

And it shall come to pass, if thou shalt hearken diligently unto the voice of the Lord thy God, to observe and to do all his commandments which I command thee this day, that the Lord thy God will set thee on high above all nations of the earth:

And all these blessings shall come on thee, and overtake thee, if thou shalt hearken unto the voice of the Lord thy God.

Blessed shalt thou be in the city, and blessed shalt thou be in the field.

Blessed shall be the fruit of thy body, and the fruit of thy ground, and the fruit of thy cattle, the increase of thy kine, and the flocks of thy sheep.

Blessed shall be thy basket and thy store.

Blessed shalt thou be when thou comest in, and blessed shalt thou be when thou goest out.

The Lord shall cause thine enemies that rise up against thee to be smitten before thy face: they shall come out against thee one way, and flee before thee seven ways.

The Lord shall command the blessing upon thee in thy storehouses, and in all that thou settest thine hand unto; and he shall bless thee in the land which the Lord thy God giveth thee.

The Lord shall establish thee an holy people unto himself, as he hath sworn unto thee, if thou shalt keep the commandments of the Lord thy God, and walk in his ways.

And all people of the earth shall see that thou art called by the name of the Lord; and they shall be afraid of thee.

And the Lord shall make thee plenteous in goods, in the fruit of thy body, and in the fruit of thy cattle, and in the fruit of thy ground, in the land which the Lord sware unto thy fathers to give thee.

The Lord shall open unto thee his good treasure, the heaven to give the rain unto thy land in his season, and to bless all the work of thine hand: and thou shalt lend unto many nations, and thou shalt not borrow.

And the Lord shall make thee the head, and not the tail; and thou shalt be above only, and thou shalt not be beneath; if that thou hearken unto the commandments of the Lord thy God, which I command thee this day, to observe and to do them:

Deuteronomy 28:1-13

But seek ye first the kingdom of God, and his righteousness; and all these things shall be added unto you.

Matthew 6:33

I go the way of all the earth: be thou strong therefore, and shew thyself a man.

And keep the charge of the Lord thy God, to walk in his ways, to keep his statutes, and his commandments, and his judgments, and his testimonies, as it is written in the law of Moses, that thou mayest prosper in all that thou doest, and whithersoever thou turnest thyself:

1 Kings 2:2,3

Envy

A sound heart is the life of the flesh: but envy the rottenness of the bones.

Proverbs 14:30

Better is the poor that walketh in his integrity, than he that is perverse in his lips, and is a fool.

Proverbs 19:1

Let us not be desirous of vain glory, provoking one another, envying one another.

Galatians 5:26

Fret not thyself because of evildoers, neither be thou envious against the workers of iniquity.

Psalm 37:1

Rest in the Lord, and wait patiently for him: fret not thyself because of him who prospereth in his way, because of the man who bringeth wicked devices to pass.

Psalm 37:7

Wrath is cruel, and anger is outrageous; but who is able to stand before envy?

Proverbs 27:4

For ye are yet carnal: for whereas there is among you envying, and strife, and divisions, are ye not carnal, and walk as men?

1 Corinthians 3:3

Charity suffereth long, and is kind; charity envieth not; charity vaunteth not itself, is not puffed up,

Doth not behave itself unseemly, seeketh not her own, is not easily provoked, thinketh no evil

Rejoiceth not in iniquity, but rejoiceth in the truth;

Beareth all things, believeth all things, hopeth all things, endureth all things.

Charity never faileth: but whether there be prophecies, they shall fail; whether there be tongues, they shall cease; whether there be knowledge, it shall vanish away.

1 Corinthians 13:4-8

Now the works of the flesh are manifest, which are these; Adultery, fornication, uncleanness, lasciviousness,

Idolatry, witchcraft, hatred, variance, emulations, wrath, strife, seditions, heresies,

Envyings, murders, drunkenness, revellings, and such like: of the which I tell you before, as I have also told you in time past, that they which do such things shall not inherit the kingdom of God.

Galatians 5:19-21

But if ye have bitter envying and strife in your hearts, glory not, and lie not against the truth.

James 3:14

Grudge not one against another, brethren, lest ye be condemned: behold, the judge standeth before the door.

James 5:9

Wherefore laying aside all malice, and all guile, and hypocrisies, and envies, and all evil speakings.

1 Peter 2:1

For jealousy is the rage of a man: therefore he will not spare in the day of vengeance.

Proverbs 6:34

Be not thou afraid when one is made rich, when the glory of his house is increased

For when he dieth he shall carry nothing away: his glory shall not descend after him.

Psalm 49:16,17

For I was envious at the foolish, when I saw the prosperity of the wicked.

Psalm 73:3

Until I went into the sanctuary of God; then understood I their end.

Surely thou didst set them in slippery places: thou castedst them down into destruction.

How are they brought into desolation, as in a moment! they are utterly consumed with terrors.

As a dream when one awaketh; so, O Lord, when thou awakest, thou shalt despise their image.

Psalm 73:17-20

Let not thine heart envy sinners: but be thou in the fear of the Lord all the day long.

Proverbs 23:17

Be not thou envious against evil men, neither desire to be with them.

Proverbs 24:1

Let us walk honestly, as in the day; not in rioting and drunkenness, not in chambering and wantonness, not in strife and envying.

But put ye on the Lord Jesus Christ, and make not provision for the flesh, to fulfil the lusts thereof.

Romans 13:13,14

For we ourselves also were sometimes foolish, disobedient, deceived, serving divers lusts and pleasures, living in malice and envy, hateful, and hating one another.

But after that the kindness and love of God our Saviour toward man appeared,

Not by works of righteousness which we have done, but according to his mercy he saved us, by the washing of regeneration, and renewing of the Holy Ghost.

Titus 3:3-5

GOD'S PROTECTION
IN YOUR HOME

Exalt her, and she shall promote thee: she shall bring thee to honour, when thou dost embrace her.

Proverbs 4:8

These things I have spoken unto you, that in me ye might have peace. In the world ye shall have tribulation: but be of good cheer; I have overcome the world.

John 16:33

He that dwelleth in the secret place of the most High shall abide under the shadow of the Almighty.

I will say of the Lord, He is my refuge and my fortress: my God; in him will I trust.

Surely he shall deliver thee from the snare of the fowler, and from the noisome pestilence.

He shall cover thee with his feathers, and under his wings shalt thou trust: his truth shall be thy shield and buckler.

Thou shalt not be afraid for the terror by night; nor for the arrow that flieth by day;

Nor for the pestilence that walketh in darkness; nor for the destruction that wasteth at noonday.

A thousand shall fall at thy side, and ten thousand at thy right hand; but it shall not come nigh thee.

Only with thine eyes shalt thou behold and see the reward of the wicked.

Because thou hast made the Lord, which is my refuge, even the most High, thy habitation;

There shall no evil befall thee, neither shall any plague come nigh thy dwelling.

For he shall give his angels charge over thee, to keep thee in all thy ways.

They shall bear thee up in their hands, lest thou dash thy foot against a stone.

Thou shalt tread upon the lion and adder: the young lion and the dragon shalt thou trample under feet.

Because he hath set his love upon me, therefore will I deliver him: I will set him on high, because he hath known my name.

He shall call upon me, and I will answer him: I will be with him in trouble; I will deliver him, and honour him.

With long life will I satisfy him, and shew him my salvation.

Psalm 91:1-16

Thou art my hiding place; thou shalt preserve me from trouble; thou shalt compass me about with songs of deliverance.

Psalm 32:7

Yea, though I walk through the valley of the shadow of death, I will fear no evil: for thou art with me; thy rod and thy staff they comfort me.

Psalm 23:4

For the eyes of the Lord run to and fro throughout the whole earth, to shew himself strong in the behalf of them whose heart is perfect toward him.

2 Chronicles 16:9a

The Lord your God which goeth before you, he shall fight for you, according to all that he did for you in Egypt before your eyes.

Deuteronomy 1:30

Hast not thou made an hedge about him, and about his house, and about all that he hath on every side? thou hast blessed the work of his hands, and his substance is increased in the land.

Job 1:10

When thou liest down, thou shalt not be afraid: yea, thou shalt lie down, and thy sleep shall be sweet.

Proverbs 3:24

When thou passest through the waters, I will be with thee; and through the rivers, they shall not overflow thee: when thou walkest through the fire, thou shalt not be burned; neither shall the flame kindle upon thee.

Isaiah 43:2

But let all those that put their trust in thee rejoice: let them ever shout for joy, because thou defendest them: let them also that love thy name be joyful in thee.

Psalm 5:11

Every word of God is pure: he is a shield unto them that put their trust in him.

Proverbs 30:5

The Lord is my rock, and my fortress, and my deliverer; my God, my strength, in whom I will trust; my buckler, and the horn of my salvation, and my high tower.

Psalm 18:2

Trust in the Lord, and do good; so shalt thou dwell in the land, and verily thou shalt be fed.

Delight thyself also in the Lord; and he shall give thee the desires of thine heart.

Commit thy way unto the Lord; trust also in him; and he shall bring it to pass.

Psalm 37:3-5

The fear of man bringeth a snare: but whoso putteth his trust in the Lord shall be safe.

Proverbs 29:25

For thou, Lord, wilt bless the righteous; with favour wilt thou compass him as with a shield.

Psalm 5:12

The angel of the Lord encampeth round about them that fear him, and delivereth them.

Psalm 34:7

God is our refuge and strength, a very present help in trouble.

Psalm 46:1

And they overcame him by the blood of the Lamb, and by the word of their testimony; and they loved not their lives unto the death.

Revelation 12:11

The thief cometh not, but for to steal, and to kill, and to destroy: I am come that they might have life, and that they might have it more abundantly.

John 10:10

But the Lord is faithful, who shall stablish you, and keep you from evil.

2 Thessalonians 3:3

If the Son therefore shall make you free, ye shall be free indeed.

John 8:36

And my people shall dwell in a peaceable habitation, and in sure dwellings, and in quiet resting places.

Isaiah 32:18

But whoso hearkeneth unto me shall dwell safely, and shall be quiet from fear of evil.

Proverbs 1:33

The Lord is nigh unto all them that call upon him, to all that call upon him in truth.

He will fulfil the desire of them that fear him: he also will hear their cry, and will save them.

The Lord preserveth all them that love him: but all the wicked will he destroy.

Psalm 145:18-20

The Lord shall preserve thy going out and thy coming in from this time forth, and even for evermore.

Psalm 121:8

Trust ye in the Lord for ever: for in the Lord Jehovah is everlasting strength.

Isaiah 26:4

O my God, I trust in thee: let me not be ashamed, let not mine enemies triumph over me.

Psalm 25:2

As for God, his way is perfect; the word of the Lord is tried: he is a buckler to all them that trust in him.

2 Samuel 22:31

GROWING IN WISDOM

I will bless the Lord, who hath given me counsel: my reins also instruct me in the night seasons.

Psalm 16:7

A wise man will hear, and will increase learning; and a man of understanding shall attain unto wise counsels.

Proverbs 1:5

Wisdom is the principal thing; therefore get wisdom: and with all thy getting get understanding.

Exalt her, and she shall promote thee: she shall bring thee to honour, when thou dost embrace her.

Proverbs 4:7,8

Counsel is mine, and sound wisdom: I am understanding; I have strength.

By me kings reign, and princes decree justice.

By me princes rule, and nobles, even all the judges of the earth.

I love them that love me; and those that seek me early shall find me.

Riches and honour are with me; yea, durable riches and righteousness.

My fruit is better than gold, yea, than fine gold; and my revenue than choice silver.

I lead in the way of righteousness, in the midst of the paths of judgment:

That I may cause those that love me to inherit substance; and I will fill their treasures.

Proverbs 8:14-21

So shall the knowledge of wisdom be unto thy soul: when thou hast found it, then there shall be a reward, and thy expectation shall not be cut off.

Proverbs 24:14

Good understanding giveth favour: but the way of transgressors is hard.

Proverbs 13:15

In the lips of him that hath understanding wisdom is found: but a rod is for the back of him that is void of understanding.

Proverbs 10:13

For I will give you a mouth and wisdom, which all your adversaries shall not be able to gainsay nor resist.

Luke 21:15

And they were not able to resist the wisdom and the spirit by which he spake.

Acts 6:10

My son, if thou wilt receive my words, and hide my commandments with thee;

So that thou incline thine ear unto wisdom, and apply thine heart to understanding;

Yea, if thou criest after knowledge, and liftest up thy voice for understanding;

If thou seekest her as silver, and searchest for her as for hid treasures;

Then shalt thou understand the fear of the Lord, and find the knowledge of God.

For the Lord giveth wisdom: out of his mouth cometh knowledge and understanding.

He layeth up sound wisdom for the righteous: he is a buckler to them that walk uprightly.

He keepeth the paths of judgment, and preserveth the way of his saints.

Then shalt thou understand righteousness, and judgment, and equity; yea, every good path.

When wisdom entereth into thine heart, and knowledge is pleasant unto thy soul;

Discretion shall preserve thee, understanding shall keep thee.

Proverbs 2:1-11

My son, forget not my law; but let thine heart keep my commandments:

For length of days, and long life, and peace, shall they add to thee.

Let not mercy and truth forsake thee: bind them about thy neck; write them upon the table of thine heart:

So shalt thou find favour and good understanding in the sight of God and man.

Trust in the Lord with all thine heart; and lean not unto thine own understanding.

In all thy ways acknowledge him, and he shall direct thy paths.

Proverbs 3:1-6

Behold, thou desirest truth in the inward parts: and in the hidden part thou shalt make me to know wisdom.

Psalm 51:6

But the anointing which ye have received of him abideth in you, and ye need not that any man teach you: but as the same anointing teacheth you of all things, and is truth, and is no lie, and even as it hath taught you, ye shall abide in him.

1 John 2:27

That the God of our Lord Jesus Christ, the Father of glory, may give unto you the spirit of wisdom and revelation in the knowledge of him.

Ephesians 1:17

And this I pray, that your love may abound yet more and more in knowledge and in all judgment.

Philippians 1:9

For this cause we also, since the day we heard it, do not cease to pray for you, and to desire that ye might be filled with the knowledge of his will in all wisdom and spiritual understanding.

That ye might walk worthy of the Lord unto all pleasing, being fruitful in every good work, and increasing in the knowledge of God.

Colossians 1:9,10

Let the word of Christ dwell in you richly in all wisdom; teaching and admonishing one another in psalms and hymns and spiritual songs, singing with grace in your hearts to the Lord.

Colossians 3:16

I wisdom dwell with prudence, and find out knowledge of witty inventions.

Proverbs 8:12

But of him are ye in Christ Jesus, who of God is made unto us wisdom, and righteousness, and sanctification, and redemption.

1 Corinthians 1:30

In whom are hid all the treasures of wisdom and knowledge.

Colossians 2:3

Who is a wise man and endued with knowledge among you? let him shew out of a good conversation his works with meekness of wisdom.

But if ye have bitter envying and strife in your hearts, glory not, and lie not against the truth.

This wisdom descendeth not from above, but is earthly, sensual, devilish.

For where envying and strife is, there is confusion and every evil work.

But the wisdom that is from above is first pure, then peaceable, gentle, and easy to be intreated, full of mercy and good fruits, without partiality, and without hypocrisy.

James 3:13-17

For after that in the wisdom of God the world by wisdom knew not God, it pleased God by the foolishness of preaching to save them that believe.

For the Jews require a sign, and the Greeks seek after wisdom:

But we preach Christ crucified, unto the Jews a stumblingblock, and unto the Greeks foolishness;

But unto them which are called, both Jews and Greeks, Christ the power of God, and the wisdom of God.

Because the foolishness of God is wiser than men; and the weakness of God is stronger than men.

1 Corinthians 1:21-25

If any of you lack wisdom, let him ask of God, that giveth to all men liberally, and upbraideth not; and it shall be given him.

James 1:5

Only by pride cometh contention: but with the well advised is wisdom.

Proverbs 13:10

Health in your home

There is that speaketh like the piercings of a sword: but the tongue of the wise is health.

Proverbs 12:18

And said, If thou wilt diligently hearken to the voice of the Lord thy God, and wilt do that which is right in his sight, and wilt give ear to his commandments, and keep all his statutes, I will put none of these diseases upon thee, which I have brought upon the Egyptians: for I am the Lord that healeth thee.

Exodus 15:26

And ye shall serve the Lord your God, and he shall bless thy bread, and thy water; and I will take sickness away from the midst of thee.

Exodus 23:25

O Lord my God, I cried unto thee, and thou hast healed me.

Psalm 30:2

Bless the Lord, O my soul: and all that is within me, bless his holy name.

Bless the Lord, O my soul, and forget not all his benefits:

Who forgiveth all thine iniquities; who healeth all thy diseases;

Who redeemeth thy life from destruction; who crowneth thee with lovingkindness and tender mercies.

Who satisfieth thy mouth with good things; so that thy youth is renewed like the eagle's.

Psalm 103:1-5

He sent his word, and healed them, and delivered them from their destructions.

Psalm 107:20

A merry heart doeth good like a medicine: but a broken spirit drieth the bones.

Proverbs 17:22

Beloved, I wish above all things that thou mayest prosper and be in health, even as thy soul prospereth.

3 John 2

My son, attend to my words; incline thine ear unto my sayings.

Let them not depart from thine eyes; keep them in the midst of thine heart.

For they are life unto those that find them, and health to all their flesh.

Proverbs 4:20-22

If my people, which are called by my name, shall humble themselves, and pray, and seek my face, and turn from their wicked ways; then will I hear from heaven, and will forgive their sin, and will heal their land.

2 Chronicles 7:14

Confess your faults one to another, and pray one for another, that ye may be healed. The effectual fervent prayer of a righteous man availeth much.

James 5:16

But if the Spirit of him that raised up Jesus from the dead dwell in you, he that raised up Christ from the dead shall also quicken your mortal bodies by his Spirit that dwelleth in you.

Romans 8:11

A merry heart maketh a cheerful countenance: but by sorrow of the heart the spirit is broken.

Proverbs 15:13

Death and life are in the power of the tongue: and they that love it shall eat the fruit thereof.

Proverbs 18:21

For he that will love life, and see good days, let him refrain his tongue from evil, and his lips that they speak no guile:

Let him eschew evil, and do good; let him seek peace, and ensue it.

For the eyes of the Lord are over the righteous, and his ears are open unto their prayers: but the face of the Lord is against them that do evil.

1 Peter 3:10-12

The young lions do lack, and suffer hunger: but they that seek the Lord shall not want any good thing.

Psalm 34:10

Who his own self bare our sins in his own body on the tree, that we, being dead to sins, should live unto righteousness: by whose stripes ye were healed.

1 Peter 2:24

The thief cometh not, but for to steal, and to kill, and to destroy: I am come that they might have life, and that they might have it more abundantly.

John 10:10

He that committeth sin is of the devil; for the devil sinneth from the beginning. For this purpose the Son of God was manifested, that he might destroy the works of the devil.

1 John 3:8

But he was wounded for our transgressions, he was bruised for our iniquities: the chastisement of our peace was upon him; and with his stripes we are healed.

Isaiah 53:5

So Jesus came again into Cana of Galilee, where he made the water wine. And there was a certain nobleman, whose son was sick at Capernaum.

When he heard that Jesus was come out of Judaea into Galilee, he went unto him, and besought him that he would come down, and heal his son: for he was at the point of death.

Then said Jesus unto him, Except ye see signs and wonders, ye will not believe.

The nobleman saith unto him, Sir, come down ere my child die.

Jesus saith unto him, Go thy way; thy son liveth. And the man believed the word that Jesus had spoken unto him, and he went his way.

And as he was now going down, his servants met him, and told him, saying, Thy son liveth.

Then enquired he of them the hour when he began to amend. And they said unto him, Yesterday at the seventh hour the fever left him.

So the father knew that it was at the same hour, in the which Jesus said unto him, Thy son liveth: and himself believed, and his whole house.

John 4:46-53

That it might be fulfilled which was spoken by Esaias the prophet, saying, Himself took our infirmities, and bare our sicknesses.

Matthew 8:17

Is any sick among you? let him call for the elders of the church; and let them pray over him, anointing him with oil in the name of the Lord:

And the prayer of faith shall save the sick, and the Lord shall raise him up; and if he have committed sins, they shall be forgiven him.

James 5:14,15

And there came a leper to him, beseeching him, and kneeling down to him, and saying unto him, If thou wilt, thou canst make me clean.

And Jesus, moved with compassion, put forth his hand, and touched him, and saith unto him, I will; be thou clean.

And as soon as he had spoken, immediately the leprosy departed from him, and he was cleansed.

Mark 1:40-42

And Jesus went about all the cities and villages, teaching in their synagogues, and preaching the gospel of the kingdom, and healing every sickness and every disease among the people.

Matthew 9:35

GOD'S DIRECTION
IN YOUR HOME

The fear of man bringeth a snare: but whoso putteth his trust in the Lord shall be safe.

Proverbs 29:25

Through wisdom is an house builded; and by understanding it is established:

And by knowledge shall the chambers be filled with all precious and pleasant riches.

Proverbs 24:3,4

For as many as are led by the Spirit of God, they are the sons of God.

Romans 8:14

The spirit of man is the candle of the Lord, searching all the inward parts of the belly.

Proverbs 20:27

For thou art my lamp, O Lord: and the Lord will lighten my darkness.

2 Samuel 22:29

Yet thou in thy manifold mercies forsookest them not in the wilderness: the pillar of the cloud departed not from them by day, to lead them in the way; neither the pillar of fire by night, to shew them light, and the way wherein they should go.

Thou gavest also thy good spirit to instruct them, and withheldest not thy manna from their mouth, and gavest them water for their thirst.

Nehemiah 9:19,20

Lead me, O Lord, in thy righteousness because of mine enemies; make thy way straight before my face.

Psalm 5:8

He maketh me to lie down in green pastures: he leadeth me beside the still waters.

He restoreth my soul: he leadeth me in the paths of righteousness for his name's sake.

Psalm 23:2,3

Lead me in thy truth, and teach me: for thou art the God of my salvation; on thee do I wait all the day.

Psalm 25:5

The meek will he guide in judgment: and the meek will he teach his way.

Psalm 25:9

Howbeit when he, the Spirit of truth, is come, he will guide you into all truth: for he shall not speak of himself; but whatsoever he shall hear, that shall he speak: and he will shew you things to come.

John 16:13

Call unto me, and I will answer thee, and shew thee great and mighty things, which thou knowest not.

Jeremiah 33:3

I will bless the Lord, who hath given me counsel: my reins also instruct me in the night seasons.

Psalm 16:7

The entrance of thy words giveth light; it giveth understanding unto the simple.

Psalm 119:130

For the Lord giveth wisdom: out of his mouth cometh knowledge and understanding.

Proverbs 2:6

Trust in the Lord with all thine heart; and lean not unto thine own understanding.

In all thy ways acknowledge him, and he shall direct thy paths.

Proverbs 3:5,6

For this cause we also, since the day we heard it, do not cease to pray for you, and to desire that ye might be filled with the knowledge of his will in all wisdom and spiritual understanding.

Colossians 1:9

If any of you lack wisdom, let him ask of God, that giveth to all men liberally, and upbraideth not; and it shall be given him.

James 1:5

Counsel in the heart of man is like deep water; but a man of understanding will draw it out.

Proverbs 20:5

Commit thy works unto the Lord, and thy thoughts shall be established.

Proverbs 16:3

When thou goest, it shall lead thee; when thou sleepest, it shall keep thee; and when thou awakest, it shall talk with thee.

For the commandment is a lamp; and the law is light; and reproofs of instruction are the way of life.

Proverbs 6:22,23

This book of the law shall not depart out of thy mouth; but thou shalt meditate therein day and night, that thou mayest observe to do according to all that is written therein: for then thou shalt make thy way prosperous, and then thou shalt have good success.

Joshua 1:8

HAVING CHILDREN

Thy wife shall be as a fruitful vine by the sides of thine house: thy children like olive plants round about thy table.

Psalm 128:3

Lo, children are an heritage of the Lord: and the fruit of the womb is his reward.

As arrows are in the hand of a mighty man; so are children of the youth.

Happy is the man that hath his quiver full of them: they shall not be ashamed, but they shall speak with the enemies in the gate.

Psalm 127:3-5

Children's children are the crown of old men; and the glory of children are their fathers.

Proverbs 17:6

The father of the righteous shall greatly rejoice: and he that begetteth a wise child shall have joy of him.

Proverbs 23:24

And all thy children shall be taught of the Lord; and great shall be the peace of thy children.

Isaiah 54:13

Correct thy son, and he shall give thee rest; yea, he shall give delight unto thy soul.

Proverbs 29:17

And God blessed them, and God said unto them, Be fruitful, and multiply, and replenish the earth, and subdue it: and have dominion over the fish of the sea, and over the fowl of the air, and over every living thing that moveth upon the earth.

Genesis 1:28

Blessed shall be the fruit of thy body, and the fruit of thy ground, and the fruit of thy cattle, the increase of thy kine, and the flocks of thy sheep.

Deuteronomy 28:4

The just man walketh in his integrity: his children are blessed after him.

Proverbs 20:7

Train up a child in the way he should go: and when he is old, he will not depart from it.

Proverbs 22:6

He is ever merciful, and lendeth; and his seed is blessed.

Psalm 37:26

But the mercy of the Lord is from everlasting to everlasting upon them that fear him, and his righteousness unto children's children.

Psalm 103:17

His seed shall be mighty upon earth: the generation of the upright shall be blessed.

Psalm 112:2

The wicked are overthrown, and are not: but the house of the righteous shall stand.

Proverbs 12:7

For I will pour water upon him that is thirsty, and floods upon the dry ground: I will pour my spirit upon thy seed, and my blessing upon thine offspring:

And they shall spring up as among the grass, as willows by the water courses.

Isaiah 44:3,4

They shall not labour in vain, nor bring forth for trouble; for they are the seed of the blessed of the Lord, and their offspring with them.

Isaiah 65:23

And I will give them one heart, and one way, that they may fear me for ever, for the good of them, and of their children after them.

Jeremiah 32:39

For the promise is unto you, and to your children, and to all that are afar off, even as many as the Lord our God shall call.

Acts 2:39

And all thy children shall be taught of the Lord; and great shall be the peace of thy children.

Isaiah 54:13

And ye shall teach them your children, speaking of them when thou sittest in thine house, and when thou walkest by the way, when thou liest down, and when thou risest up.

Deuteronomy 11:19

And these words, which I command thee this day, shall be in thine heart:

And thou shalt teach them diligently unto thy children, and shalt talk of them when thou sittest in thine house, and when thou walkest by the way, and when thou liest down, and when thou risest up.

And thou shalt bind them for a sign upon thine hand, and they shall be as frontlets between thine eyes.

And thou shalt write them upon the posts of thy house, and on thy gates.

Deuteronomy 6:6-9

And, ye fathers, provoke not your children to wrath: but bring them up in the nurture and admonition of the Lord.

Ephesians 6:4

And God Almighty bless thee, and make thee fruitful, and multiply thee, that thou mayest be a multitude of people.

Genesis 28:3

PART II

DEVOTIONS FOR YOUR MARRIAGE

Day 1
Understanding Your Partner

Wisdom is the principal thing; therefore get wisdom: and with all thy getting, get understanding.

Proverbs 4:7

Having been pastor of several churches, I have met many people who thought their mates should be perfect, while they themselves treated their mates like slaves.

We must understand that our marriage companion is not perfect, cannot be perfect, and will never be perfect.

Don't try to make your companion live up to a standard that he or she can never reach; after all, you are not perfect either.

Prayer: Father, give me understanding. Help me to understand that my wife or husband can never be perfect. Help me not to try to force him or her into a mold that is impossible to live up to. In the name of Jesus, I pray.

Adapted from *A Daily Guide to a Better Marriage* by Donald E. Moore (Tulsa: Harrison House, 1983).

DAY 2
THE EXAMPLE OF LOVE

Charity never faileth.

1 Corinthians 13:8

When a person becomes angry or confused, he has a tendency to try to force or drive, rather than to lead with love. You may be trying to force your mate into changing instead of loving him or her into changing.

The word *charity* used in this verse means love, a giving love. When we think of charity, we think of giving. Sometimes in a marriage if we look real closely at ourselves, we might see that we have slipped out of an attitude of giving love into one of a driving, forcing, "you-will-do-it-or-else" kind of attitude.

Prayer: Father, help me to lead my mate with love. Help me not to drive or force, but to love and lead by setting the example I should. In the name of Jesus, I pray.

Day 3
Help, not criticism

Put away from thee a froward mouth, and
perverse lips put far from thee.

Proverbs 4:24

I find that most people spend more time
complaining than helping. If you will be honest
with yourself, you may find that you are
complaining all the time about what your mate
is doing wrong, instead of helping him or her to
do it right.

Many times we find ourselves spending more
time helping strangers than we do our own
family. You must take time to work with your
own loved ones. Take time to teach and help each
other.

Even ministers fall into this trap. A pastor
may help or teach others, but does he take the
time to minister to his own wife or children?

I hear many men say, ''I wish my wife knew
the Bible like So-and-So's wife does.'' My
question to them is: Have you taken the time to
teach your wife, or only to complain?

*Prayer: Father, help me to take the time to teach
my own family, not harping or complaining, but
helping them through their weaknesses. In the name
of Jesus, I pray.*

A D<small>AY</small> 4
A WORD FITLY SPOKEN

A word fitly spoken is like apples of gold
in pictures of silver.

Proverbs 25:11

In dealing with others, we must remember
that a right attitude often makes the difference
between success and failure. People can feel what
comes from your spirit, whether good or bad,
love or hate.

Think before you speak. Is what you are about
to say to your mate a fitly spoken word? Is it in
the right attitude?

What you say, and how you say it, may well
determine whether you convince your mate you
are sincerely trying to help him or her to
overcome a weakness.

*Prayer: Father, help me to have the right attitude
toward my mate. Help me to choose fitly spoken words,
words of love and kindness. In the name of Jesus, I
pray.*

Day 5
Trouble Not Yourselves

He that troubleth his own house shall inherit the wind....

Proverbs 11:29

When two people are joined together in marriage, the Bible says that they become one flesh. (Gen. 2:24.) When you fight against your marriage partner, you hurt your own self.

You will never win by taking the world's attitude of ''I'll get even with you.'' You must understand that if you hurt your companion, you are destroying part of yourself.

As a result of fighting and bickering, homes end in divorce and the family gains nothing. Rather, it loses everything.

Prayer: Father, help me not to trouble my own house. Help me to love my mate. In the name of Jesus, I pray.

Day 6
Forgive and forget!

> And above all things have fervent charity
> (love) among yourselves: for charity (love) shall
> cover the multitude of sins.
>
> 1 Peter 4:8

For a real breakthrough to come in your marriage, you must learn to forgive and to forget all of your partner's past failures and mistakes.

We sometimes find this hard to do because there are some things we simply don't want to forgive and forget. Sometimes we have gotten the mistaken idea that we need to hold on to our mate's past failures and mistakes to use as a weapon against him or her in time of argument.

No marriage will ever succeed until the partners learn to forgive as Christ forgave. How did He forgive? He forgave — and forgot! Remember, "Love never fails." The weapon with which you are going to win the battle is not a carnal or fleshy weapon, but rather it is with love that you can win the victory.

Prayer: Father, help me to forgive and forget as you do, so that there may be healing in our marriage and room in our hearts and minds for a fresh start. In the name of Jesus, I pray.

Day 7
The love of god

> But God commendeth his love toward us,
> in that, while we were yet sinners, Christ died
> for us.
>
> Romans 5:8

Sometimes after we have been hurt or bruised, we find it hard to let go of old wounds. If you are finding at this point that it is hard to forgive and forget, then you need to review the Scriptures on what Christ did for you.

> But he was wounded for our transgressions,
> he was bruised for our iniquities: the
> chastisement of our peace was upon him; and
> with his stripes we are healed.
>
> Isaiah 53:5

Christ died for you while you were still a lost sinner. God sent his love through Jesus Christ while you did nothing but sin against Him. He loved you with all your problems.

Prayer: Father, help me to show my wife or husband the same love with which You loved me. In the name of Jesus, I pray.

Day 8
By Faith, Not Feelings

For we walk by faith, not by sight.
2 Corinthians 5:17

At this point your flesh (your feelings) may not be happy at the decision you have made to forgive and forget by faith.

You cannot build a marriage on feelings; it must be built on the Word of God. You can never build a strong marriage on feelings. A marriage is a lifetime commitment. You need to commit yourself to win over the devil, and to save your marriage.

Prayer: Father, help me to put away my childish feelings and build my marriage on the written Word of God by faith. In the name of Jesus, I pray.

DAY 9
COMMITMENT IN MARRIAGE

> Your adversary the devil, as a roaring lion,
> walketh about, seeking whom he may devour.
> 1 Peter 5:8

There must be a strong commitment to build a marriage because the devil has come to destroy. He tries to divide a house against itself, because he knows it will not stand if the members are not united as one against him.

We must understand that we have to work harder than the devil. We must cast down the works of Satan in the name of Jesus.

Prayer: Father, help me to stay committed to working harder at our marriage. In the name of Jesus, I pray.

Day 10
The Power of Prayer

Confess your faults one to another, and pray one for another, that ye may be healed. The effectual fervent prayer of a righteous man availeth much.

James 5:16

There is nothing that can take the place of praying in faith for the person you are trying to win.

When a person prays, he gets God involved on the scene. Sometimes we don't pray for our marriage partners as much as we think we do. We pray many hours for everybody else, and everything else, forgetting to spend the needed time to pray for our own husband or wife, the one with whom we live the most intimately and upon whom we depend every day.

Prayer: Father, help me to spend time in prayer for my husband or wife. Help me to reach down in my heart and pray in faith for him or her. In the name of Jesus, I pray.

Day 11
They two shall be one

For this cause shall a man leave his father and mother, and shall be joined unto his wife, and they two shall be one flesh.

Ephesians 5:31

Most people spend so much of their time earning a living that they forget to live.

Yes, we do need to work, but we also need to spend time with our families. This is vitally important to a heathy home and marriage. We need time together, to get to know the needs of each other. We need to fulfill that deep desire in the heart of our marriage partner that can only be filled by us alone.

There is a certain fellowship I can share with my wife that she cannot get from anyone else. This was ordained by God, as it was He who joined man and wife together.

Prayer: Father, help me to take time to love my wife or husband, and help me to take time to share with him or her. In the name of Jesus, I pray.

Day 12
First Things First

> But seek ye first the kingdom of God, and
> his righteousness; and all these things shall be
> added unto you.
>
> Matthew 6:33

"I don't have time." We hear that statement
spoken nearly every day of our lives. Perhaps you
have said it yourself thousands of times. "I don't
have the time to spare for my family."

You will never have time; you will have to
make the time. The devil knows that if he can get
you to neglect your family long enough, it will
fall apart. I learned a number of years ago that
if a person doesn't take the time needed for his
family, it will never come.

If you will ask God, He will help you to find
time. It will seem as if more hours have been
added to the day, or your work will be done
faster, or you will see that other things are just
not that important.

*Prayer: Father, help me with my time, so that I
can be with my family as I should. In the name of Jesus,
I pray.*

Day 13
Say the Good Word

Heaviness in the heart of man maketh it stoop: but a good word maketh it glad.

Proverbs 12:25

Whom do you remember and appreciate the most? Isn't it the person who tries to build you up and not tear you down?

We all need to be built up, not brought down. Everyone needs to be encouraged. We all need to be commended. This will go a long way toward building up a great marriage.

Most husbands and wives are too busy criticizing each other. Soon, so much criticism turns into hate and rebellion.

Your words of encouragement will create a closer unity in your marriage. It will take time, but if you will begin to speak words of encouragement and commendation, through patience you will begin to see the Holy Spirit at work in your marriage.

Prayer: Father, help me to build up my marriage, and not to tear it down by speaking words of discouragement. Give me words inspired by the Holy Spirit to speak to my mate. In the name of Jesus, I pray.

DAY 14
PATIENCE

For ye have need of patience, that, after ye have done the will of God, ye might receive the promise.

Hebrews 10:36

You may discover at this time there is still a lot of work to be done in your family, even in your own self.

This is nothing to get discouraged about, rather rejoice that you see the truth and are willing to change. Sometimes, if you will look closely, you will find that your patience with your family is shorter than with people outside your home. This should not be. If there is anyone we should love, have patience with, be willing to teach and work with, it is our own family. If you can be kind to others, you can be kind to your own family members. Put Philippians 4:13 to work: "I can do all things through Christ which strengtheneth me."

Prayer: Father, I repent of my lack of patience, of not trying as hard to work with my own family as I do with other people. In the name of Jesus, I pray.

Day 15
Give yourselves to prayer

But we will give ourselves continually to prayer....

Acts 6:4

The greatest thing you can do for your marriage and family is to pray for them continually, not just when you feel like it, or when there is a family crisis. Your marriage and family needs the covering of prayer on a daily basis.

In the original Greek, the phrase, *to give ourselves continually*, is one word with two roots: 1) *pros*, meaning "toward, in the direction of, forward, or pertaining to," and 2) *kartero*, meaning "endurance, strength, steadfastness, and power." The word, *proskartero*, can be defined as "persevering diligence, or steadfast earnestness."

Giving oneself continually to prayer means taking prayer seriously, making the time and energy and commitment to prayer. Make the commitment to pray for your marriage and family continually.

Prayer: Father, help me to give myself continually to prayer on behalf of my marriage and family. In the name of Jesus, I pray.

SDAY 16
SOURCE OF LOVE

And hope maketh not ashamed; because the love of God is shed abroad in our hearts by the Holy Ghost which is given unto us.

Romans 5:5

You may say, ''I find it hard to love my husband or wife.''

It is good that you admit to a wrong in your life, but through God that situation can be changed.

Love is in your heart. You may not feel it, but it is there nonetheless. It may be suppressed, but you can activate it by confessing that the Holy Spirit has put love in your heart.

Prayer: Father, help me to have a new love in my heart for my mate and family. In the name of Jesus, I pray.

GDAY 17
GET IN AGREEMENT

Can two walk together, except they be agreed?

Amos 3:3

A lot of problems in marriage can be worked out if only the couple is willing to talk and then really listen to each other. A husband and wife should always be willing to talk things out.

But it is not enough just to talk, they must be willing to listen to each other, keeping an open mind about what is said.

I have seen people whose minds were already closed before I could talk to them. This can only block the working of God. Learn to listen, then be willing to pray and to follow the leadership of God's Holy Spirit in your marriage.

Prayer: Father, help me to be willing to talk and listen to my wife or husband, and then help me to seek Your face in prayer and to be willing to do whatever You show me to do. In the name of Jesus, I pray.

Day 18
Show Appreciation

The lips of the righteous know what is acceptable: but the mouth of the wicked speaketh frowardness.

Proverbs 10:32

One thing that many married people fail to do is to look for new ways to improve themselves, their mate and their marriage.

When a couple first meet, they go out of their way to be nice and polite to each other. But after they have been married for a while, they begin dropping their guards. They start taking each other for granted. They forget to compliment each other.

A lot of hard work goes into making and keeping a home (caring for children, earning the living, washing dishes, mowing the grass, cleaning the house, keeping the cars clean and in good running order, doing the laundry, etc.) Learn to appreciate all the things your mate does for you and compliment him or her on it.

Prayer: Father, help me to appreciate my wife or husband for all the good things he or she does for me. In the name of Jesus, I pray.

Day 19
Friendship in Marriage

Go home to thy friends....

Matthew 5:19

A person's best friends should be in his own home. Far too many married couples fail to learn how to be each other's best friend.

But friendship must be developed. Proverbs 18:24 says, "A man that hath friends must show himself friendly." Do you know how to win new friends? The Bible says you must show yourself friendly.

I have found that couples who not only love one another, but who also are each other's best friends, invariably have a marriage that is strong and enjoyable. They are able to confide in and have confidence in one another. They enjoy each other's company.

Prayer: Father, I ask you to help me not only to build love in our marriage, but also friendship. Help me to show myself friendly toward my mate. In the name of Jesus, I pray.

Day 20
Make decisions together

If a house be divided against itself, that
house cannot stand.

Mark 3:25

Married couples need to make decisions
together as partners, understanding that major
decisions will affect the whole family.

Resentment, even hatred, will sometimes
build up in one of the partners because he or she
is left out of decision making. Some husbands
and some wives, for example, will go out and buy
things on credit, not consulting with their mate
first, not thinking whether they can afford what
is being charged or not, getting the family into
debt. Such action can only lead to arguments and
bitterness.

Too many couples will not spend the time
needed together in prayer before a decision is
made. If family decisions are based on the Word
of God, they will be good for the entire family.

*Prayer: Father, help me to take the time to involve
my companion in my actions. Let us pray about the
decisions we make. In the name of Jesus, I pray.*

DAY 21
JEALOUSY

For jealousy is the rage of a man: therefore
he will not spare in the day of vengeance.

Proverbs 6:34

Jealousy is a rage. Husbands and wives need
to beware of this dreadful enemy. Do not let it
into your lives. Learn to trust each other; have
faith in each other. This will build a stronger
marriage.

I have seen men and women destroy beautiful
marriages because of a jealous heart. Satan will
talk to a person and put thoughts in his or her
head that are not so. I have seen men get mad
if they saw their wives talking to another man,
even though the conversation was purely
innocent.

My wife knows that as a minister I have to
talk with other women all the time, but there is
a trust there. As a minister's wife, she has to deal
with all kinds of people, so we have both learned
to trust each other, knowing that our work is for
the glory of the Lord.

*Prayer: Father, help me to rebuke the enemy of
jealousy and to cast it out of my heart. In the name
of Jesus, I pray.*

SDAY 22
SET THE EXAMPLE

We then that are strong ought to bear the infirmities of the weak, and not to please ourselves.

Romans 15:1

In a marriage, the stronger should set the example for the other to follow.

From my years of experience in counseling, I have seen that many times in a marriage there is one partner who tried hard, while the other partner does not seem to really care. If this is your case, you must not give up. You must realize that you are fighting a spiritual warfare with the devil. God is on your side. You can win; but you must be willing to obey the instructions of God and pay the price for a better marriage. Part of that price is setting the example for your mate to follow.

Prayer: Father, help me to set an example for my marriage. Help me to pay the price to build a better marriage. In the name of Jesus, I pray.

Day 23
Cast down imaginations

> Casting down imaginations, and every high thing that exalteth itself against the knowledge of God, and bringing into captivity every thought to the obedience of Christ.
>
> 2 Corinthians 10:5

"The harder I try, it seems the worse our marriage becomes. Why try?"

If this expresses your feelings, you must cast such thoughts down. They are from Satan. The devil wants to build up in your mind the imagination that you cannot win, that there is no hope, no use in trying.

This is a direct attack upon the Word of God. God said, "Love never fails." If God has said something, you can count on it; it works. Keep on fighting the good fight of faith. You can take your marriage out of the hands of the devil. You can win because God is on your side.

Prayer: Father, help me to cast down imaginations, and to take on the mind of a winner. I can do all things through Christ who strengthens me. In the name of Jesus, I pray.

Day 24
Fight the Good Fight

But thanks be to God, which giveth us the victory through our Lord Jesus Christ.

1 Corinthians 15:57

Anything worth having is worth fighting for, and every marriage is worth having. But wishing and hoping and daydreaming will not get the job done. By using your faith and not giving up, you will see results.

If you think that the devil is going to sit still while you build a marriage that will glorify God, you are wrong. If my wife and I had not been willing to pay the price for success in the early years of our marriage, we would not have a marriage today. The devil threw everything he had at us, but praise God we were more than conquerors through Christ our Lord.

Prayer: Father, help me to use my faith; help me to take authority over the enemy who is trying to destroy our marriage. In the name of Jesus, I pray.

A Day 25
Accentuate the Positive

Finally, brethren, whatsoever things are honest, whatsoever things are just, whatsoever things are pure, whatsoever things are lovely, whatsoever things are of good report, if there be any virtue, and if there be any praise, think on these things.

Philippians 4:8

Find the good things in your marriage and mate, look for the best and not for the worst. You may say, "But there is nothing good in the person that I have married." Sometimes through a period of time, a person begins to see only the negative side and not the positive. You will usually find what you are looking for, if you look long and hard enough. If you look for faults, you will find them, because no person and no marriage is perfect.

Begin to look for the good things in your marriage and mate. The more you look, the more you will find.

Prayer: Father, help me to look and think on the good things in our marriage. In the name of Jesus, I pray.

Day 26
The God-Kind of Love

There is a friend that sticketh closer than a brother.

Proverbs 18:24

God sees deep down on the inside of us. He sees all of our mistakes, all of our faults. But He still loves us and wants our fellowship.

This is one of the greatest revelations I have ever received. God knows all about me, but He still loves me and wants to fellowship with me. It goes even deeper than that. Romans 5:8 says, While we were yet sinners, Christ died for us. If Almighty God, a perfect and upright God, so loved us, knowing all about our sins and faults, how much more should we be willing to love and forgive one another?

Husbands and wives need this God-kind of love in their homes.

Prayer: Father, help us to have Your kind of love for each other. Help us to have the God-kind of love. In the name of Jesus.

Day 27
The Undefiled Bed

Marriage is honourable in all, and the bed undefiled; but whoremongers and adulterers God will judge.

Hebrews 13:4

The marriage bed has been ordained by God to enrich the love and fellowship of each marriage. But many marriages are destroyed or never have the rich enjoyment that God has intended, because people sometimes think sex is dirty. Yet it was God Who created and ordained sex. But He reserved it exclusively for man and his wife.

A husband and wife can never be at perfect peace unless there is a good sex life between them. There is a hunger in each heart that can only be filled by this part of marriage.

Prayer: Father, help me to yield my life to this part of Your plan for a man and wife; help me to fulfill the need in my mate's life. Help us to close the door to the devil so that he cannot take advantage of a weak link in our relationship. In the name of Jesus, I pray.

Day 28
Ravished with Love

Let her be as the loving hind and pleasant
roe; let her breasts satisfy thee at all times; and
be thou ravished always with her love.

Proverbs 5:19

Here are instructions from God concerning
the sexual relationship in a marriage. Notice these
words: loving, pleasant, satisfy, ravished.
Obviously sex plays a great part in marriage,
whether a person wants to admit it or not.

Learn to be concerned about your mate's
sexual need. It is your responsibility to fulfill that
need always and at all times. You may say, ''But
he (or she) will take advantage of me.'' No, your
submission will cause your love for each other
to grow; and where love grows, fellowship and
consideration will also grow.

A husband and wife must learn to satisfy each
other by their love for one another, and sex is one
way in which that love is nurtured and increased.

*Prayer: Father, help me not to have the wrong
attitude about our sex life, but let this be a pleasant
time of fellowship together. In the name of Jesus, I
pray.*

226

Day 29
Defraud not the other

The wife hath not power of her own body, but the husband, and likewise, also the husband hath not power of his own body but the wife.

Defraud ye not one the other, except it be with consent for a time, that ye may give yourselves to fasting and prayer; and come together again, that Satan tempt you not for your incontinency.

1 Corinthians 7:4,5

It is unscriptural for a husband and wife to withhold sex from each other. The Word of God says that they should refrain only with consent, and then only for a time of fasting and prayer. Afterwards they should come together again so that Satan will not tempt them.

I have counselled with couples who were using sex as a weapon against each other to get even about something. Such people always end up in arguments and with heartaches. Look at sex in the marriage as pure and undefiled. Work together to build a healthy sex life.

Prayer: Help us to love each other, to fulfill each other's needs as You have commanded. Help us to build a better marriage. In the name of Jesus, I pray.

DAY 30

WISDOM

If any of you lack wisdom, let him ask of God, that giveth to all men liberally, and upbraideth not, and it shall be given him.

James 1:5

We must understand that marriage must be founded upon the Word of God. It must be built upon a proper relationship between the marriage partners and with God.

Don't give up on your marriage. Get God involved in your problems. He has the wisdom you need, and will give it to you. He will not hold back anything from you.

You must remember that God wants to help you and your marriage be a total success. To pull your marriage out of difficulty will take time. You must be patient and let God help you each day.

Prayer: Father, I ask You to give me wisdom and insight about how to build a better marriage each day. In the name of Jesus, I pray.

Part III
Prayers for Your Marriage

PRAYER FOR OUR LIFE TOGETHER

Father, it is written in Your Word that love is shed abroad in our hearts by the Holy Ghost Who is given to us. Because You are in us, we acknowledge that love reigns supreme. We pray that love is displayed in full expression, enfolding and knitting us together in truth, making us perfect for every good work to do Your will, working in us that which is pleasing in Your sight.

We pray that we will live and conduct ourselves and our marriage honorably and becomingly. We esteem it as precious, worthy, and of great price. We commit ourselves to live in mutual harmony with one another delighting in each other, being of the same mind and united in spirit.

Father, help us to be gentle, compassionate, courteous, tender-hearted, and humble-minded. Help us to bear with each other and forgive whatever grievances we may have against one another. We will forgive as the Lord forgave us.

We pray that our marriage will grow stronger day by day in the bond of unity, rooted and grounded in Your love. Father, we thank you in Jesus' name. Amen.

Husband's Prayer

Lord, I pray that love and faithfulness will never leave us, that we will bind them about our necks and write them on the tablets of our hearts so that we will win favor and a good name in the sight of God and man.

Lord, I make You my confidence, and I will trust in You for our Safety. Your instruction is far more valuable than silver or gold.

I pray that our lives together will bear fruit, the good fruit of winning souls.

Help me to be thoughtful of my wife's needs and to respect her as a partner and an heir with me in the gracious gift of life, so that my prayers will not be hindered.

Help me to not be self-seeking, proud, or easily angered, but patient, loving and kind toward my wife. I pray that my wife and I will be of one mind, united in spirit, compassionate, courteous and tenderhearted to each other.

Thank You, Lord, for my wife. I receive her as a wonderful blessing from You. In Jesus' name I pray. Amen.

Wife's Prayer

Lord, help me to comfort, encourage and do my husband only good as long as there is life within me. Grant me wisdom to look over my home. I pray for strength and spiritual, mental, and physical fitness for my God-given tasks.

My heart will trust and be confident in You, Lord, and I will not fear or dread evil. Help me to be patient, tenderhearted, loving and kind toward my husband, dwelling in unity with him.

I pray our marriage will grow stronger every day, that we will delight in one another, forgiving one another freely as God in Christ has forgiven us.

I pray You will always keep love in our hearts — forever being thankful that you brought us together in this holy union. In Jesus' name I pray. Amen.

Part IV
Selected Poems

HOW DO I LOVE THEE?

How do I love thee! Let me count the ways.
I love thee to the depth and breadth and height
My soul can reach, when feeling out of sight
For the ends of Being and ideal Grace.
I love thee to the level of everyday's
Most quiet need, by sun and candle-light.
I love thee freely, as men strive for Right;
I love thee purely, as they turn from Praise.
I love thee with passion put to use
In my old griefs, and with my childhood's faith.
I love thee with a love I seemed to lose
With my lost saints, — I love thee with the breath,
Smiles, tears, of all my life! — and, If God choose,
I shall but love thee better after death.

— *Elizabeth Barrett Browning*

OUR LORD DIRECTS OUR WAY

God does not lead us year by year
    Nor even day by day,
But step by step our path unfolds,
    Our Lord directs our way.

Tomorrow's plans we do not know,
    We only know this minute.
But He will say, "This is the way,
    By faith now walk ye in it."

And we are glad that it is so;
    Today is ours to share,
And when tomorrow comes, His grace
    Shall far exceed its care.

What need to worry then or fret?
    The God who gave His only Son
Holds all our moments in His hand
    And gives them one by one.

— *Author unknown*

IF THOU MUST LOVE ME

If thou must love, let it be for naught
Except for love's sake only, Do not say
"I love her for her smile — her look — her way
Of speaking gently, — for a trick of thought
That falls in well with mine, and certes brought
A sense of pleasant ease on such a day" —
For these things in themselves, Beloved, may
Be changed, or change for thee — and love, so
  wrought,
May be unwrought so. Neither love me for
Thine own dear pity's wiping my cheeks dry:
A creature might forget to weep, who bore
Thy comfort long, and love thy thereby!
But love me for love's sake, that evermore
Thou mayest love on, through love's eternity.

— *Elizabeth Barrett Browning*

A RED, RED ROSE

O, my luve is like a red, red rose,
   That's newly sprung in June.
O my luve is like the melodie
   That's sweetly played in tune.

As fair art thou, my bonnie lass,
   So deep in luve am I,
And I will luve thee still, my dear,
   Till a' the seas gang dry.

Till a' the seas gang dry, my dear,
   And the rocks melt wi' the sun!
And I will luve thee still, my dear,
   While the sands o' life shall run.

And fare thee weel, my only luve,
   And fare thee weel awhile!
And I will come again, my luve,
   Though it were ten thousand mile!

               — *Robert Burns*

GROW OLD ALONG WITH ME

Grow old along with me!
The best is yet to be,
The last of life, for which the first was made:
Our times are in his hand
Who saith, ''A whole I planned,
Youth shows but half; trust God: see all, nor be
   afraid!''

— *Robert Browning*

Song

How many times do I love thee, dear?
  Tell me how many thoughts there be
    In the atmosphere
    Of a new-fall 'n year,
Whose white and sable hours appear
  The latest flake of Eternity: —
So many times do I love thee, dear.

How many times do I love again?
  Tell me how many beads there are
    In a silver chain
    Of evening rain,
Unravelled from the tumbling main,
  And threading the eye of a yellow star: —
So many times do I love again.

— *Thomas Lovell Beddoes*

Shall I compare thee

Shall I compare thee to a Summer's day?
Thou art more lovely and more temperate:
Rough winds do shake the darling buds of May,
And Summer's lease hath all too short a date:
Sometime too hot the eye of heaven shines,
And often is his gold complexion dimm'd;
And every fair from fair sometime declines,
By chance or nature's changing course
   untrimm'd:

But thy eternal Summer shall not fade
Nor lose possession of that fair thou ow'st;
Nor shall Death brag thou wander'st in his shade,
When in eternal lines to time thou grow'st:
So long as men can breathe, or eyes can see,
So long lives this, and this gives life to thee.

— *William Shakespeare*

A ROSE NEEDS LOVE

A Rose without water will wither.
A Rose without sunlight will fade.
And the Rose without love and attention
Will not live even one day.

So don't take the love that is given
And crush it and throw it away
For words that are spoken harshly
Will cause love to die all the way.

So speak softly to your darling
With tenderness and care,
For the Rose that you so wanted will
   bloom to its fullest,
And will grow deeper for you each day.

For in giving your best to your loved ones,
And caring for what they have to say,
You're saying, "Darling, I love you,"
In one of the most precious ways.

Jesus said, "Love one Another,"
And without this love we will die,
So water your Rose carefully,
And plant it deep in the love of God's ways.

— *A.L. Fiasconaro*

DREAM HOUSE

Living with my bride in a castle on a hill,
Just for this moment all time stands still.
I see her in the garden picking roses in the sun,
Together at last, the waiting is done.

Lying on the hillside, reclining in the grass,
Time stands still as eternities pass,
Staring at the clouds in the sky of deep-sea blue,
Nothing to disturb us in this world for two.

I feel her warmth beside me,
I stop and wonder why
I received this treasure
From my Father in the sky.

I lean over to caress her
And to look into her eyes,
And then from deep within me
Comes the answer to my "whys."

I realize the Father God, Who formed my inmost
    parts,
Is the same and very God Who joined both our
    hearts.
So instead of wasting all my time
By questioning my life,

I will live life to its fullest,
And share it with my wife!

— *Steve Lynch*

PART V

KEYS FOR SUCCESS

IN MARRIAGE

Six Keys to Marital Happiness

By Tim LaHaye

Many a time I have wished I were a magician! When a married couple tells me their problems and resultant miseries, I would love to wave a magic wand over them and watch them leave my office to ''live happily ever after.''

Naturally, I don't have such a wand. But I do have six keys that are guaranteed to open the door to a happy marriage. Examine each key carefully. The degree to which you use them determines the success of your marriage. If you neglect them, your marriage cannot help but be a miserable and wretched experience. These keys come from the Bible, God's manual on human behavior. Therefore, I can guarantee happiness and success to all who use them.

Key No. 1: Maturity

The first key that guarantees happiness in marriage is maturity. This key is best defined in the emotional realm as unselfishness. Babies and small children are selfish — thus we refer to them as immature. When a child throws a fit in a super-

---

Excerpted from *How To Be Happy Though Married* by Tim LaHaye (Wheaton: Tyndale House, 1968). Used by permission.

market by lying on the floor, screaming, and kicking his feet because he can't have his way, he is revealing his selfishness or immaturity.

If such a child is not properly disciplined, he will go into marriage so immature that he will want his own way in practically every situation. Such an attitude, very subtle and difficult for the immature person to recognize, is disastrous to a marriage.

The Problem

The adjustment stage of marriage, usually considered the first three years, will naturally produce conflicts of interest. For the first twenty or more years of their lives, people function as independent gears. They make decisions purely on the basis of what they want or what is good for them. After the wedding, two independent individuals must learn to mesh together. Since they are both moving objects, and all movement creates friction, there is bound to be friction as they learn to move together in unity.

This friction is illustrated in the old-fashioned transmission. As long as the car was standing still without the motor running, you could move the gear shift, meshing different gears at will, without problems. Once in motion, it was quite a different matter. It was not uncommon to hear these moving gears "clash" as the car was shifted in an effort to increase its speed. Automobile manufacturers solved this problem some years ago by installing a "synchromesh gear." This gear makes possible the bringing together of two or more moving gears in unity without "clashing."

The synchromesh gear in marriage is unselfishness. If two mature people come together in marriage, their spirit of selflessness will make it very easy for them to adjust. If they are immature and selfish, the early years of their marriage will be filled with "noisy clashes."

Marriage consists of a series of actions and reactions motivated by our conscious and subconscious minds. The more active the people, the more potential the areas of conflict can be expected. Conflict, however, need not be fatal. In fact, some counselors suggest that conflicts are normal and can provide a creative force in marriage.

Dr. Alfred B. Messer, addressing the American Psychiatric Convention in October of 1966, said, "A spirited spat is good for most marriages.... Arguments are inevitable in a marriage and probably offer one of the best ways couples have to work out touchy problems. When most of the frustrations have been talked out or discharged in some vicarious way, the fight can be ended. Those marriages that exist without any type of fighting are generally frozen or inflexible marriages in which other aspects of the relationship are compromised in order to maintain the facade of peace and harmony.''

Although some conflict is inevitable between two normal human beings, fighting is not necessarily the answer. By God's grace, two mature people can face their areas of conflict, discuss them, and by obeying the injunctions of God's Word resolve them. Don't get into the habit of sweeping your problems under the rug. Face them and resolve them in the spirit. Actually, there is nothing wrong with having a conflict of interest between husband and wife. In fact, every such case is a test of your maturity. The partner that demands ''his own way'' in such conflicts is traveling a collision course that will produce much unhappiness for both of them.

You Never Get By Getting

After I completed a marriage counseling session some years ago, the prospective bride looked at me and said, ''Your advice is sure different from the advice the girls at the office gave me. They said, 'Bonnie, one thing to remember in marriage is that men are out for all they can get. Don't give too much of yourself to your husband; he'll just take advantage of you.'''' That unchristian and unsound attitude is one of the things that produces so much misery in American homes.

In God's economy, you never get anything by getting. The way to have something is to give it away. If you want love, for example, don't look for it — give it. If you want friends, don't look for friends — be friendly. The same is true of thoughtfulness, consideration and selflessness. If you want your partner to treat you unselfishly, then be mature enough by God's grace to treat him unselfishly.

Why did you get married in the first place? The answer to that question may give you insight into your maturity. Did you get married because "I had an unhappy home life" or because "I got tired of my parents' telling me what to do" or because "All of my friends were getting married and I didn't want to be left alone" or because "I wanted somebody to love me"? The proper attitude that guarantees success in a marriage is based on mature unselfishness. Mature individuals will go into marriage not only for what they can get out of it, but for what they can give to their partners. Two verses in the Bible come close to being a magic wand; when used by marriage partners, they turn chaos into peace and harmony:

> Let nothing be done through strife or vainglory; but in lowliness of mind let each esteem other better than themselves.

> Look not every man on his own things, but every man also on the things of others.
> Philippians 2:3-4

If you go into marriage with this attitude — "look not on your own things...but on the things of your partner" — you will discover happiness in your home. Your attitude should never be that it is your partner's responsibility to make you happy. You must initially recognize your responsibility to make your partner happy.

There is an irrelevant and erroneous saying about marriage that has somehow become popular: Marriage is a fifty-fifty proposition. Nothing could be further from the truth! Marriage, under God, should be a one-hundred-percent-to-nothing proposition. That is, you should go into your marriage with the idea that you are going to give yourself for the purpose of making your partner happy and expect nothing in return. The result will be your own happiness. Your desire in marriage should be to make your partner happy. Of course, if you do that you will reap happiness in return.

A sharp young couple came to see me some years ago with conflict written all over their marriage. George had come from a very secure home. His greatest pleasure was to go hunting with his father on weekends. Ellen came from a very insecure home where her parents' many conflicts produced an early desire for her to get married and get away from it all. After four years of marriage they discovered that their love was not destroyed, but they were at such cross

254

purposes that they knew that it soon would be if something were not done.

I soon discovered that they both were disappointed in the results of their marriage. They had entirely different concepts of married life. Ellen, who was inclined to escape the nasty realities of now by dreaming about a Utopian future, wanted marriage to be a "blissful time of relaxation and family life, particularly on weekends."

George thought marriage should be a relaxed home life five nights a week, with most weekends spent hunting and fishing with his father and some day, he hoped, with his son. In fact, he wanted to get married as soon as he did because he spent so much time with Ellen while courting her that he had to give up some of his treasured hunting experiences.

Strangely enough, they both knew what the problem was; they just had never faced it before. Every time he planned a trip with his father, Ellen would become angry, and they would exchange cutting remarks. When she crawled into her self-protective shell of silence and frigidity, it was even worse. Sometimes he couldn't enjoy the hunting trip, because he knew things were not right at home.

Fortunately, these two people were mature enough to face the fact that their marriage was more important than "togetherness" or hunting trips. We worked out an agreement in which they would both give in to the other's desires on this matter. George went on only half as many hunting trips and Ellen tried hard to send him out of town in a good spirit. Several times she didn't feel very good about it, but for his sake she tried vigorously and succeeded.

Then one day a friend invited them to go water skiing. Both were excellent swimmers, and they took to this form of entertainment like ducks take to water. A few weeks later they bought a boat and now regularly go out on Saturdays with friends for an enjoyable time together.

Was it a great sacrifice for George? When I asked him some months later how things were going, he replied, ''For some reason I've lost a lot of my interest in hunting and fishing. I only go three or four times a year now. I would rather go water skiing with Ellen, or do something else with her and the children.'' Don't be afraid of giving in. All you will do is win in the long run.

Selfishness Is Universal

Selfishness, the greatest single enemy to a happy marriage, is a basic part of man's fallen nature. The important thing to remember is that something can be done to overcome selfishness.

The Bible tells us in 2 Corinthians 5:17, ''Therefore if any man be in Christ, he is a new creature: old things are passed away; behold, all things are become new.'' The Greek construction of this verse indicates the gradual passing away of old things, which includes man's natural selfishness. When Jesus Christ comes to live in a person's life, he creates a new nature within him that, if yielded to and nurtured, will overpower the old nature.

How To Overcome Selfishness

Selfishness can be corrected by the power of God in conjunction with a cooperative individual. God will give you the power if you are willing to cooperate with him. The following steps are highly successful in changing selfish behavior into unselfish acts of thoughtfulness towards others.

• Face your selfishness as a sin! Until you are able to recognize your selfishness as a sin displeasing to God and to others, you will never be able to think of others before you think of yourself. Too many people excuse it on the basis that ''I was given a free hand by my parents, and I just developed the habit of doing whatever I want.'' The fact that your parents made the mistake of indulging you by not limiting your activities to those areas that were good for you is no reason to perpetuate that mistake for a lifetime. Instead, face it as a sin.

• Don't try to hide behind academic or economic success to cover your selfishness. Maturity is relative. That is, a man may be a brilliant scientist and a good leader at work, but a selfish, overgrown baby as a husband at home. A woman may be an effective organizer and women's club president or church worker, but a selfish, childish, miserable wife. Face the truth that no matter what you are in the business or academic world, if you fail in your marriage, you have failed in an important area of your life. Selfishness is the greatest cause of marital failure.

• Once you have faced the fact that your selfishness, regardless of your partner's behavior, is a sin before God, you have made a giant step. Before you will submit to an operation, your doctor must convince you that you have a disease or some other physical malady. Excusing the symptoms will never correct the problem.

The same principle applies in the emotional realm. As long as you cover up your selfishness, excuse it, or ignore it, you will never correct it. Happy is the man who understands that he, and he alone before God, is responsible for his actions and reactions, and that when he acts with a selfish motive he has sinned against God as well as against his fellow man.

• Confess your selfishness as a sin. There are no big sins or little sins in God's sight. Sin is sin. Whenever you act selfishly, be sufficiently objective about yourself to confess your sin to your heavenly Father, then be assured that he will forgive you. (1 John 1:9.)

• Ask God to take away the habit of being selfish. "And this is the confidence that we have in him, that, if we ask any thing according to his will, he heareth us: And if we know that he hears us, whatsoever we ask, we know that we have the petitions that we desired of him" (1 John 5:14-15). Since it is not God's will that we be selfish creatures, he will direct us in changing our habit of behaving selfishly.

• Repair the damage done by your selfishness. Whether or not he deserves it, apologize to whomever you exhibited your immaturity or self-seeking and you will find it easier and easier to avoid selfish behavior. A person soon learns that he would rather not be selfish because it is harder to humble himself enough to say, "I was wrong. Will you forgive me?" than to give up selfish behavior.

• Repeat this formula every time you do or say something under the motivation of selfishness. It will help you become a happy, well-adjusted, and unselfish person whose company other people enjoy. In addition, your maturity may gradually inspire maturity in your partner. Before you realize it, the key of maturity will open many doors to happiness in your marriage.

Key No. 2: Submission

No organization can function properly if it has two heads. That is particularly true of the home.

One of the great hindrances to a happy home today is the false notion that a woman does not have to subject herself to her husband. Modern psychology and education seem to give women the idea that subjection is an old-fashioned notion that went out with the nineteenth century. But when subjection goes out of the home, so does happiness.

Today we have more frustrated women, men and children than ever before. With the down-grading of the father image and the rising dominance of the mother role we have witnessed an increase in juvenile delinquency, rebellion, homosexuality and divorce.

God intended man to be the head of his home. If he is not, he will not have a sense of responsibility but will subconsciously feel he is married to a second mother. His children will soon detect who is boss, and as teenagers they will lose the natural respect for their father that is necessary for their adjustment to life.

Usually a wife-dominated home is a quarrelsome home until the husband finally "gives up." He then crawls into his shell of introversion and degenerates into a sub-par human being.

The sad thing is, a wife will eventually grow to despise the husband she dominates.

A Command of God

The Christian woman must be in subjection to her husband! Whether she likes it or not, subjection is a command of God and her refusal to comply with this command is an act of disobedience. All disobedience is sin; therefore, she cannot expect the blessing of God on her life unless she is willing to obey God. The following Scripture passages establish this fact.

Unto the woman he said, I will greatly multiply thy sorrow and thy conception; in sorrow thou shalt bring forth children; and thy desire shall be to thy husband, and he shall rule over thee.

Genesis 3:16

Wives, submit yourselves unto your own husbands, as unto the Lord.

For the husband is the head of the wife, even as Christ is the head of the Church: and he is the savior of the body.

Therefore as the church is subject unto Christ, so let the wives be to their own husbands in every thing.

Ephesians 5:22-24

. . .and the wife see that she reverence her husband.

Ephesians 5:33

Likewise, ye wives, be in subjection to your own husbands; that, if any obey not the word, they also may without the word be won by the conversation of the wives;

261

While they behold your chaste conversation coupled with fear.

1 Peter 3:1,2

The refusal of many Christian wives to accept the principle of subjection is increasingly common today. A number of years ago I taught a Bible class of forty-five adults — twenty-three women and twenty-two men. I gave the results of the curse of Genesis 3 on the man, the woman, and the ground and the serpent. Concerning the woman, I pointed out that she had two parts to her curse: one, sorrow in childbirth; two, being ruled over by her husband. The next week I gave an examination and believe it or not, in response to the question, ''What was the result of the curse to the woman?'' I received twenty-three female answers: She shall have sorrow in childbirth. The twenty-two men answered: She shall be ruled by her husband. A few of the men also included that she would have sorrow in childbirth. The fact that not one of those twenty-three women, who voluntarily attended that Bible class for the purpose of spiritual growth, had remembered the subjection part of the curse illustrated to me the universal tendency of women to reject this God-given command.

God's Tool for Your Happiness

God never commands people to do that which is impossible or is not for their good. The Holy Spirit has asked in Romans 8:32, ''He that spared

262

not his own Son, but delivered him up for us all, how shall he not with him also freely give us all things?'' The answer to that is, if God loved us so much that He gave His Son to die for us, certainly He will give us all those things that are for our good. Therefore, by faith accept the fact that submission to her husband is for a woman's good.

Somewhere between thirty-five and forty-five a woman usually reaches a period when she increasingly desires to become a leaner. If she is aggressive in the early years of marriage and dominates her husband, she teaches him to lean on her. Then, when she gets to the age where she wants a man to lean on, she finds that she has created a leaner and has no one on whom she can lean. I've seen many a woman at this stage come to loathe the man whom she, in her younger years, trained to be a docile, submissive spouse.

It is safe to assume that dominating wives have caused great misery in marriage, both to themselves and to their partners. The woman who enjoys bossing her husband when she is twenty-five may find life turning into a nightmare as she advances in age. It is an act of faith in a Christian woman's heart to assume that for her lasting happiness and the happiness of her husband, it is essential that she be obedient to God and put herself in subjection to her husband.

Subjection Is Not Slavery

When a Christian woman seeks God's grace and the filling of the Holy Spirit to enable her to live in subjection to her husband, she is not in danger of becoming a slave. Many times I have seen women seek to be subjected for spiritual reasons only to find that the reaction in their husband has been one of thoughtfulness and kindness which caused a cessation of hostilities between them. Usually a woman finds that she fares far better when she is in subjection than when she dominates. Certainly she will enjoy a better walk with God when she is obedient to her husband for the Lord's sake, than when she disobeys God by dominating her husband.

Subjection does not mean that a woman can't voice her opinion by "speaking the truth in love" (Eph. 4:15), but that she should seek to be submissive to her husband's desires when he reaches a decision and that she comply with his requirements whenever humanly possible. There may be times when she will have to do something that she really doesn't want to do, but by sowing the seeds of obedience on that matter she will reap the harvest of blessing on many others.

Always remember, you reap far more than you sow. If you sow submission in obedience to God, you will reap blessing in abundance; if you sow rebellion in disobedience to the will of God, you will reap abundant misery. Some women have a

264

more aggressive temperament than their husbands, and admittedly it is more difficult for them to be in subjection. In fact, the only way I know they can is to recognize that it is a spiritual responsibility. When this fact has been established in her mind, any woman can summon the grace of God to be the submissive person God wants her to be.

Some years ago I counseled with a woman who was far more aggressive than her husband and found that through the years, even though he was well-educated, she had made the major decisions of the family. When the children came in to ask questions, he would be relaxed and quiet while she answered and made decisions. At about thirty-five years of age she recognized that he was gradually receding into a shell of compliance in the home and she was assuming dictatorial powers. When she became convinced of her need to submit to her husband for the Lord's sake, she asked God to help her bite her tongue and stifle her intuitive inclination to make spontaneous decisions — and to wait for her husband to make the decision.

She was amazed to find that in a brief period of time he rose to the challenge and gradually assumed the decision-making prerogatives in the home. Interesting to me as I counseled with this woman was the fact that the more she submitted, the more he led; the more he led, the happier she was; and the happier he was, the happier she was. That marriage was gradually changed from the point of living together because they were Christians to a new spark of genuine love and respect for each other. To me, this couple is a living example of the fact that a wife's submission to her husband is a key to a happy marriage.

Key No. 3: Love

The third key that guarantees a happy marriage is love. Probably no other word is more misunderstood in the English language than this one. Most people today do not know what love is. They often confuse physical attraction, lust, personal desire, sympathy, or compassion with love. Love is one of the most common experiences of man and one of the most difficult to define. Webster defines it as "a feeling of strong personal attachment induced by sympathetic understanding, or by ties of kinship; ardent affection."

The Bible says the love of a husband for his wife should equal his love for himself. God instructed him to love his wife sacrificially as Christ loved the Church and gave himself for her (the Church). No woman can be unhappy when given that kind of love, and the husband who gives that kind of love will be the recipient of sacrificial love.

Like God, love cannot be seen, but we know of its existence because of its effects. It is easier to describe love than define it. Although many have attempted a description of love, in all the annals of literature there is none that compares with those masterful words that come from the pen of the Apostle Paul in the great love chapter, First Corinthians 13:4-7:

> Charity suffereth long, and is kind; charity envieth not; charity vaunteth not itself, is not puffed up.

> Doth not behave itself unseemly, seeketh not her own, is not easily provoked, thinketh no evil;

> Rejoiceth not in iniquity, but rejoiceth in the truth;

> Beareth all things, believeth all things, hopeth all things, endureth all things.

Henry Drummond, in a book entitled, *The Greatest Thing in the World,* points out the nine characteristics of love found in this preceding passage: patience, kindness, generosity, humility, courtesy, unselfishness, good temper, guilelessness, and sincerity. Study these characteristics and examine your love to see if it meets God's standard of acceptable expression.

These nine expressions of love communicate the love of one human being to another in terms that are meaningful to everyone, regardless of race or background. No one will naturally express his love in all of these characteristics. Some people are patient and kind by nature, but lack humility, generosity or confidence. Others are naturally sincere and courteous, but lack a good temper and are prone to be impatient. All men need the power of the Holy Spirit to supply the kind of love God expects us to extend to our partners. The Holy Spirit gives the Christian (Gal. 5:22,23) the ability to express complete love.

The love that God requires of a husband for his wife and the wife for her husband is admittedly a supernatural love. Self-preservation is the first law of life; therefore, to love someone else as your own body demands a supernatural kind of love. It is just not possible for man to love this way of his own accord. However, since God never commands us to do that which He will not enable us to do, we can call upon Him, the author of love, and know that He will supply us with that kind of supernatural love. The Bible tells us, ''Beloved, let us love one another, for love is of God, and every one that loveth is born of God and knoweth God'' (1 John 4:7).

Both husband and wife are commanded to love each other, but it should be pointed out that while the wife is commanded once (Titus 2:4) to love her husband, the husband is commanded at least three times to love his wife (Eph. 5:25,28,33). The reason is probably that women by nature have a greater capacity for love.

Love Is Kind

One of the primary characteristics of love is kindness. Somehow, many of those having trouble in marriage have forgotten to show kindness. They want to receive it, but they forget to give it. A couple who had been married two years came in to see me, fulfilling the promise that I require of all young couples before marriage that before they separate from each other, they come and talk the matter over with me.

They were ready to call it quits even though they sensed they had a little love left in their marriage. The problem was, they were very caustic, sarcastic, and cutting in their speech toward each other. When this was revealed in counseling, I gave them the assignment of memorizing the nine characteristics of love and, since kindness to each other was conspicuously absent, I asked them to give their conversation "the kindness check." That is, every time they said something to each other they were to ask themselves, "Was that kind?" If not, they were to apologize and seek God's grace to be kind. Obviously, it was difficult for a time, but within two months this couple had reoriented themselves to the point that they could be kind to each other and the result was a renewing of their genuine affection for each other.

269

Love Shows Approval

Most psychologists agree that the basic needs of man are love and approval. The more we love someone, the more we naturally seek his approval. For that reason, if a person does not express his love by showing approval occasionally, he will have a dissatisfied mate.

A couple came to see me one time that were complete opposites physically. The man was six-feet-four and weighed at least 235 pounds — a real football type. The woman could not have weighed over 105 pounds and was probably about five feet tall. In the course of counseling, he said in an emotion packed voice, "Pastor, I haven't hit that woman in all the years we have been married," and as he said it he doubled up his gigantic fist. I looked at her, and saw tears running down her cheeks as she dejectedly said, "That's true, but many times I wish he had hit me instead of everlastingly clubbing me with disapproval!"

I honestly believe that disapproval is a more vicious way of inflicting punishment upon another human being than physical abuse. And the sad part is, the thing people disapprove of in their partner is usually blown up out of proportion, making the problem greater than it is.

Many a man would have to admit that he has a good wife, and the thing that aggravates him comprises only ten to fifteen percent of the total person. His problem is that he has concentrated too much on the negative instead of thanking God for the positive. It is good to frequently ask yourself, ''Do I express approval of my partner?'' That approval should be expressed both publicly, to assure your friends that you love your partner, and privately. Many a man has been given a neater house by commending his wife for those areas that are neat rather than condemning her for those that are messy. Be sure of one thing, your partner needs your approval for his or her adjustment in life and marriage. Most people respond better to commendation than to condemnation.

Love Can Be Rekindled

''I just don't love my husband anymore!'' said a young woman whose husband was not a Christian. She was looking for the wrong way of escape — divorce. Not loving your partner does not necessarily testify to the unloveliness of the partner, but it does reveal your own lack of love. God will give you love for your partner if you seek it! As we have already seen, love is of God. (1 John 4:7.) If you want to love your partner, you can! God has commanded you to love him, or her, and He will enable you to if you ask Him. In fact, the first characteristic of the spirit-filled life is ''love'' (Gal. 5:11). If you find your love beginning to wane, then go to your heavenly Father, the author of love, and He will give you a new love for your partner.

It is yours for the asking! You may be inclined to ask, ''But is it worth it?'' or ''What if my partner doesn't deserve it?'' That has nothing to do with it. You should love your partner for the Lord's sake; but, because of the principle of reaping what you sow, loving will bring you love. If you go to God by faith for his supply of love to give to your partner, then God's divine law will bring love to you.

The young woman previously mentioned prayed with me for that kind of love, and God gave it. Just the other night after a service she said to me, ''You just wouldn't believe the way God has returned my love for my husband! In fact, he has never been more loving and considerate in the eight years we have been married.''

Women Respond to Love

I never cease to marvel at the endurance of a woman's love. Women have told me things about their husbands that could earn them the title, ''the meanest man in town,'' yet these women end up by saying, ''but I still love him.'' Men would never put up with some of the things that most women are forced to endure. It must be a carry over of a mother's love which we tend to think of as the greatest illustration of human love. Whatever the cause, I am convinced that a woman has a far greater capacity to love a man than a man has to love a woman. I have yet to see a woman who will not respond to love.

No man in his right mind would present himself as an authority on women. Most of us say they are complex creatures and they are. Like other men, I do not claim to be an authority on feminine matters, but after counseling several hundred of the so-called ''weaker sex'' I have come to one basic conclusion. Most American men do not know how to make a woman happy. I have learned that it isn't money, diamonds, furs, houses, or other things that make a woman happy, but just plain love. Not lovemaking, but the treatment that produces lovemaking — kindness, thoughtfulness, understanding, acceptance or approval, and the recognition on the part of the husband that he is just not complete without her.

Happy is the wife whose husband knows and tells her that if given the chance to marry all over again, he would choose the same bride. Whenever a man tells me, ''My wife doesn't love me anymore,'' I immediately know that he is a man who has not loved his wife ''as his own body.'' If he had, she would return his love — that's just the nature of women.

Key No. 4: Communication

Young lovers rarely have a communication problem! They seem to be able to talk about

273

anything. Somehow, the ability often vanishes after they are married.

Lack of communication is almost always a problem for the couples who come to me for marriage counseling. If it is not lack of communication, it is wrong communication. Communicating under pressure of anger and shouting at the top of one's voice is the wrong approach. This is communication that could well be omitted in every marriage. Problems and differences in a marriage are not dangerous — not being able to communicate the differences, or problem areas, is dangerous. As long as two people can keep the lines of communication open and freely express their feelings, differences can be resolved.

The following statement by Ann Landers in her syndicated column illustrates the importance of communication. ''The most important single ingredient in a marriage is the ability to communicate. If my mail is a fair reflection of what goes on with Mr. and Mrs. America behind closed doors (and I think it is), most marital problems stem from the inability of two people to talk to each other. How precious is the ability to communicate! . . . The mature man and woman recognize that there is a unity in love, but at the same time there must be freedom for both individuals. Neither should be swallowed up by the other. Each must maintain his personality and his identity. A sound marriage should mean togetherness, but it also should mean respect for the rights and privileges of the other party. The couples who are secure in marriage can be honest about all kinds of feelings. . . . The man and wife who can air their differences, get the hostility out of their system, then kiss and make up have an excellent chance of growing old together.''

It has been amazing to me to find that many couples settle for a second-rate marriage relationship primarily because they have never learned to communicate. A few years ago a woman, who did not know I already had talked with her husband, came to me for counseling. Their problem seemed to be that the woman was not completely committed to the Lord. But her lack of commitment to Christ was not the real problem. A few weeks later she gave me a ride home after a meeting and spontaneously invited me in to talk to both of them. Her husband was surprised, but quickly responded; and suddenly I was acting as a referee between two friends.

For twenty minutes she calmly mentioned some of her pet gripes and objections to her husband. None of them were unusual or severe but added together created a spirit of resentment in her. Some things went back to within six months after they were married. When she finished, he very calmly said to her, ''Honey, why in the world didn't you tell me these things years ago?'' (They had been married ten years.) Her answer was, ''I was afraid to. I thought you would explode.''

Knowing that every argument has two sides, I asked the husband if he would like to voice his objections to her as kindly as he could. For a similar period of time he then rehearsed her weaknesses and when he finished, she turned and said, ''Why didn't you tell me this before?'' He replied, ''Because I thought you would get mad and go into a long period of silence.'' By learning to communicate, that couple soon learned to exchange their honest feelings without fear and the wife was able to fully commit herself to Christ.

Communication Killers

How does the wall of resistance to communication gradually build up between two people who love each other? Naturally, neither plans the erection of such a wall; it gradually grows from the time of their first breakdown in communication. Dr. Henry Brandt shared with a group of ministers the three weapons that people use to defend themselves. As you look at these three weapons, you will find that by using them married people gradually build a wall of resistance so they are no longer able to communicate.

The first weapon is *explosion*. Whenever a person is told his shortcomings, rather than face them honestly, his natural reaction is to explode. This explosion is the result of inner anger and hostility that causes him to attempt self-protection. What this does is teach our partner that "you can't come that close to my intimate weaknesses; if you do, I'll explode."

The second self-defense weapon that hinders communication is *tears*. This weapon is used mostly by women, though sometimes men will resort to it. Like the other weapons, it is a way of saying to your partner, "Don't tell me my shortcomings, or I'll cry!" The first spat after marriage often leaves the bride in tears. This teaches the new husband that she has a breaking point and subconsciously he will thereafter tend to hold back his communication lest he make her cry. Thus, another brick is laid in the wall that stifles communication.

A parenthetical note is appropriate here on feminine tears. Husband, learn to distinguish between your wife's tears of emotion, stress, joy and self-pity. Women are far more intricate creatures than men, and often show their emotions through tears.

Don't despise your wife's tears! Be patient and kind, for the emotional creature you married is just being a woman. In fact, I have found that the woman who is easily moved to tears has the greatest capacity to express her emotions in every area of life.

Usually that type of wife is more responsive to tenderness and lovemaking than the dry-eyed girl. In fact, years ago I came to the conclusion that women who weep easily are seldom frigid, and tearless wives often have emotions like an iceberg. Since that time I have counseled more than one thousand women and have had no reason to change my conclusion.

If your wife is emotionally expressive, thank God! Her tears testify to this emotional richness that makes her a compassionate mother and loving wife. Be particularly thoughtful during her menstrual period, as she may be unusually emotional then. "Tender loving care" (TLC) during that period is like laying up treasure in heaven — it pays off by and by.

The third weapon is *silence*. Silence is the weapon that many older Christians learn to use. It is not long before we realize that it isn't Christian to get mad and explode all over the neighborhood when our partner crosses us or points out our weaknesses. Then, too, as children come along, we are reluctant to weep in front of them. Therefore, Christians resort to silence.

Silence, however, is a very dangerous tool. It is dangerous in that it rapidly stifles communication and takes a heavy toll physically and spiritually upon a person. It takes tremendous power to be silent for a long period of time; anger can supply that power. Since anger is one of the leading causes of ulcers, high blood pressure and many other diseases, you will find that silence is a very expensive tool to use on your partner.

Some years ago, I counseled with a couple and one of their problems was that the man was very slow of speech and his wife was just the opposite. Whenever he would try to express himself, she couldn't wait but would give the rebuttal to his statement before he had finished. In fact, her constant chatter often reminded me of a machine gun as she blasted away at him. He soon learned that he was no match for her in an argument.

One day I met him at church and just casually asked, "How are things going?"

"Wonderful," he said. "I finally found out to handle that woman!"

When I asked him how he did it, he said, "Through silence. The one thing she can't stand is for me to be silent. When she crosses me I will go for long periods without talking. In fact, I even went five days one time without speaking to her."

My answer to him was, "That is going to be a very expensive tool, because pent-up anger and bitterness produce ulcers." Little did I realize how prophetic my statement was, for in a matter of weeks, I got the report that he had a bleeding ulcer.

How much better it would be if two people would learn to freely communicate their differences, and thereby avoid not only problems but also the side effects. Remember, all anger, bitterness, and wrath grieve the Holy Spirit. (Eph. 4:30-32.) No man can walk in the Spirit and be mad at his wife. (Gal. 5:16.)

How To Communicate

The Bible teaches that we should "speak the truth in love..." (Eph. 4:15). One should bear in mind, however, that the more truth you would speak, the more love you should use in conveying that truth. Truth is a sharp two-edged sword, so use it carefully. When you have an area in your marriage that needs communication, consider using the following steps in presenting your case.

• Pray for the wisdom of God and the filling of the Holy Spirit. When you seek God's wisdom you may find that your objection to your partner's behavior is not really valid. Or, you may sense the leading of the Spirit of God to go ahead and communicate your problem.

• Plan a time that is good for your partner. Usually you should not discuss anything of a serious or negative nature after 10:00 or 10:30 p.m. Life tends to look darker and problems loom greater at night. However, if your partner is not an early riser, the morning is not the best time either.

Many couples find that after supper is a good time for communication. Small children can often make this less than desirable, but each couple should find a time when they are in the best possible mood to look objectively at themselves.

• Speak the truth in love — in kind words say exactly what is on your heart. Make sure that your love is equal to your truth.

• Don't lose your temper. Wise couples determine early in their marriage that they will not raise their voices at each other. Under anger we often say more than we intend and usually this excess is cutting, cruel and unnecessary. Anger on one person's part usually precipitates an angry response by the other. Kindly state your objection in love but state it only once, then trust the Holy Spirit to use your words in effecting a change.

• Allow for reaction time. Don't be surprised if your communication is met with an explosive reaction, particularly in the earlier stages of marriage. Remember, you have the advantage in that you know what you are going to say; you have prayed it over and have been able to prepare yourself — your partner is taken by surprise. Don't defend yourself, but let your partner think about what you have said. He may never admit that you are right, but usually you will find that it will create a change in his behavior and after all, you are more interested in that than you are in verbal agreement.

• Commit your problem to God. Once you have told your partner, you have done about all you can do, humanly speaking, to change his behavior. From that point on, you must trust God either to help your partner change his objectionable habit or to supply you with the necessary grace to live with it. (2 Cor. 11:9.)

Two Golden Expressions

There are two golden expressions that every married couple should communicate to their partner repeatedly throughout their marriage.

I'm sorry. Everyone makes mistakes. Romans 3:23 points out that "all have sinned, and come short of the glory of God." You will sin against your partner and your partner will sin against you many times in a normal marriage. If, however, you are willing to face your mistakes and apologize to your companion, you will find resistance dissolve and a spirit of forgiveness will prevail. If you are unwilling to acknowledge your mistakes, then you have a serious spiritual problem — pride.

One time I counseled with a couple and the wife tearfully said, "My husband has never apologized to me in the twenty-three years we have been married." Turning to him, I asked him if he had ever done anything wrong. He quickly replied, "Oh, of course, I am only human." I then asked, "Why have you never apologized?" His reply was, ''I didn't think it was very manly for me to apologize; my father never apologized to my mother.'' Unfortunately, this man grew up under a father who made a very terrible decision never to apologize. Now this man was perpetuating that mistake and reaping the resultant misery. When you are wrong, face it objectively and honestly admit it — both to yourself and to your partner.

I love you is the second golden expression in a marriage. I have already pointed out that it is absolutely necessary for every human being to be loved. Your partner will never tire of hearing you tell him or her of your love. This expression of love seems to be more meaningful to women than men, but I am inclined to believe women are just more prone to admit the need for it, and that men need it also.

A man came in to see me the day after his wife of fifteen years had left him. He was a brilliant engineer with an I.Q. of 148, he said, and made an excellent salary. As he told me about the shipwreck of his marriage, he acknowledged that he had not told his wife he loved her for ten years. When I asked him why, he said, ''Why should I have to tell her? I have demonstrated it faithfully for fifteen years. She didn't like the house we lived in, so I bought her another house. She didn't like her car, so I bought her another car to run around in. She didn't like the carpeting, so I had it taken out and new carpeting put in. If I didn't love her would I have given her five children?''

The amazing thing about the whole affair was that his wife had run off with a sailor who made a very small salary and looked enough like her husband to be his twin brother. In exasperation he said to me, ''What could that poor sailor possibly give to my wife that I haven't already given her?''

My answer was, ''Just one thing, love.''

As brilliant a scientist as he was, this man was an ignoramus as a husband. Their problem could have been absolved if he had been willing to give of himself and let her know that he loved her and approved of her. He couldn't seem to understand that although saying ''I love you'' sounded childish to him, it was meaningful to her. Nor did he understand that if he had not been so selfish he would have been more than willing to express in words what she wanted to hear. The more your partner loves you the more he enjoys hearing you express your love. Say it meaningfully and say it often.

Key No. 5: Prayer

Keys to a happy marriage would not be complete if I did not include prayer. Prayer to their heavenly Father is the best means of communication between two people. Many a marriage has been completely transformed by initiating a practice of regular prayer.

One method I heartily recommend is conversational prayer. I learned this method from an article in King's Business. My wife and I inaugurated this method with a slight modification and have found it to be a tremendous blessing. Here is how it works: each night one person leads the prayer time by praying for one subject at a time. The other partner then prays for the same subject. The first one then prays for the next burden of his heart and his partner again prays for the same thing. This procedure is continued until they have prayed for about five to ten things.

The next night it is the other partner's turn to initiate prayer burdens and thus by praying specifically for the burden of the other person's heart, it isn't long before they are both burdened for the same thing. My wife and I found that after a few weeks we couldn't always remember who had a burden first, but came to identify ourselves with each other's burdens. Another blessing we discovered was that in prayer we were reminded to share things that we had forgotten to share because of the busy activities of life. This sharing further broadens the common bond that exists between a husband and wife.

Having reached a stalemate with two of the couples I was counseling, I decided to ask them to try this method of prayer. One couple started that very night, and within a week called to say they didn't feel they needed to come in for counseling anymore because the "Lord has solved our difficulties." The other couple refused to enter into this prayer relationship and though many months have passed it is quite apparent they are still living in an "armed truce."

Someone has said, "You can't quarrel with the woman you have prayed with every day." There is something humbling about getting down on your knees together; it is emotionally beneficial to both parties. Many a couple has acknowledged they rise from their knees more genuinely intertwined than before they prayed. Try it and see.

Who should initiate prayer? Ordinarily the husband, the head of the home; but if he doesn't, the wife can. The time spent in prayer together can very well be the most valuable time of your lives. Don't wait until the complexities of life drive you to your knees. If you wait until some difficulty arises to pray together, you will find that when you need God most you know Him least. Learn to know Him together in prayer now so that when life's pressure is on, you can go in prayer to one you already learned to know as a close friend.

Key No. 6: Christ

Things equal to the same thing are equal to each other is a well-known geometric principle. If two people are properly related in a personal way to Jesus Christ, they will most likely be properly related to each other. Jesus Christ wants to be Lord and Savior of you as an individual. Then, he wants to be the Lord of your marriage. If he is, then the home you are building will abide in lasting peace and blessing. If he is not the spiritual head of your home, you will find that you will never experience all of the blessing that God has for you in marriage. Jesus said, "Without Me ye can do nothing" (John 15:5).

If you have never received Jesus Christ, may I suggest that right now you bow your head and invite him into your life. He said, "Behold, I stand at the door and knock: if any man hear my voice, and open the door, I will come in to him, and will sup with him, and he with me" (Rev. 3:20). If you desire Him to come into your life, all you need do is ask Him.

Once inside, He then, by His Spirit, will direct you in all areas of life, and will "supply all your need."

The test of all marital behavior in relationship to Christ should be, "Is it done with His approval?" The Scripture teaches, "And whatsoever ye do in word or deed, do all in the name of the Lord Jesus, giving thanks to God and the Father by him'' (Col. 3:17). Jesus Christ is interested in every area of your life: physical, emotional, financial, and spiritual. Living in accordance with His will as revealed in His Word, is the most important thing you can do to insure a happy marriage. You can then say:

Christ is the head of this house,

The unseen guest at every meal,

The silent listener to every conversation.

Without a doubt, Christ is the greatest key to happiness in marriage.

If you ask God to help you utilize these six keys in your life and marriage, your home will become increasingly blessed and happy.

TEN COMMANDMENTS FOR A HEALTHY MARRIAGE
By Richard Exley

1. *Protect your day off at all costs and spend it together, as a couple, and as a family.* If an emergency makes it impossible at your regular time, reschedule another day immediately.

2. *Eat dinner together.* This is a time for sharing and making memories. Issues can be dealt with at another time.

3. *Go to bed together.* Nothing undermines intimacy faster than separate bedtimes.

4. *Don't hold a grudge.* The only hope for marriage lies in the ability to forgive and forget. Don't let past hurts rob you of today's joy.

5. *Don't take separate vacations.* Shared experiences bond you together.

6. *Never let anything rob your marriage of the sexual joy God intended.* Sex is a gift from God to be enjoyed in marriage. While true intimacy is certainly more than sex, it is never less than that.

7. *Pray together.* It is often threatening at first, but the rewards more than justify the effort.

8. *Play together.* The capacity for playfulness is often a mark of a good marriage.

9. *Little things mean a lot.* In fact, they can make the difference between a mediocre marriage and a really good one.

10. *Pledge yourselves, not only to physical faithfulness, but to emotional fidelity as well.* Do not allow friends, family or career to supply these ''belonging needs.''

Part VI
Your marriage ceremony

WEDDING TRADITIONS

A wedding, traditionally, is the happiest single occasion in the life of a man and woman, with the possible exception of the birth of a child. That happiness includes joy, excitement, and the expectancy that comes with standing on the threshold of a great adventure. A wedding also is a solemn occasion. Whether a large or small event, the ceremony is supposed to be a binding covenant, a contract between two people for life. This is true, whether the wedding is religious or a civil ceremony.

Over the years of recorded history, different peoples have invested the wedding ceremony with various customs and rituals that — for a particular culture — have enhanced the solemnity and added to the rejoicing at the birth of a new union. Some of those customs have found their way into the "melting-pot" culture of the United States.

However, many couples probably have never even considered why some of these customs exist. Yet, the history of wedding customs is a very interesting one. In the following pages, some of these customs are explained and described.[1]

Everyone has heard an old adage concerning the bride's apparel that goes like this: "Something borrowed, something blue; something old, something new.''

The **"something borrowed"** is supposed to bring a blessing with it from the person to which the item belongs.

"Something blue": This tradition comes from ancient Israel, when brides wore blue borders on the fringes of their robes. Blue symbolically stood for modesty, fidelity (loyalty), and love, also purity.

"Something old": The old item was worn to show the connection between the past and the future, the joining of two families, two lines of genealogy into a new connection. It also stood for established values, for tradition.

"Something new": The new partnership was to be symbolized by the wearing of a new item of clothing or an accessory which the bride had bought — or which had been given to her — especially for the occasion. This also symbolized the expected prosperity of the couple.

The bride wore white: That phrase is still a common line in any news coverage of the majority of weddings. Why does the bride wear white?

Since Roman times white has been a symbol of celebration. In the 1800s, a white bridal outfit also was a sign of affluence. Less well-to-do brides usually had to choose a gown or dress that would serve for Sunday wear for the next few years, possibly a shade of purple, such as mauve or lavender, or a shade of gray.

Even black dresses were sometimes chosen, because in those days a black dress was considered appropriate for every occasion. In fact, in some areas of Spain, the bride wore a black silk dress and black lace mantilla, a combination of veil and cape draped over a headdress. The groom's shirt was embroidered by the bride.

Around the turn of the century, white became accepted instead of blue as a symbol of purity. After World War I, most wedding gowns in this country have been white.

The wedding ring: A ring not only suggested unending love through its circular shape, it also was an emblem of authority. Up until the days of World War II, the ring was a symbol of delegated authority, a symbol of favor, in the Middle East.

Today's double-ring ceremony denotes a loving submission to one another's welfare and well-being, as well as a symbol of love. In primitive times, the wedding ring was of vegetation that could be twisted into a rope ring and had to be replaced each year. The ancient Romans wore rings of iron, as a symbol of the expected longevity of the union. Today, gold, silver or platinum rings are chosen for their beauty and value, as well as for the symbolic and traditional values.

The ring is worn on the third finger of the left hand because people used to believe that the vein in the third finger was directly connected to the heart. In the Middle Ages, the custom was for the bridegroom to place the ring on three of his bride's fingers during the wedding ceremony to denote the blessing of the Father, Son, and Holy Spirit on the union. The ring remained permanently on the third finger.

In some European countries, the wedding ring is worn on the left hand during the engagement but switched to the right at the marriage ceremony.

The bridal veil: A veil is seldom worn in modern weddings — except as part of the more elaborate gowns. The veil is a remnant left from the days when women did not show their faces in public, since only a husband was supposed to see the face of a woman. In the western world, it has been thousands of years since women wore veils to hide their faces from men in everyday life.

Usually wedding veils are transparent and are only symbolic of the fact that a woman's innermost being is only to be viewed by her husband. Some books of marriage customs say the veil symbolizes youth and virginity. One legend is that Martha Washington's granddaughter started the American fashion of wearing a veil by wearing a long lacy scarf over her head and shoulders at her wedding.

Allegedly, her fiance, an aide to President Washington, gave her the idea when he complimented her after seeing her through a lace curtain at her home.

Giving away the bride: The custom of the bride being escorted to the altar by her father, who at one point in the ceremony ''gives'' her away, dates back to the days when women had very few personal rights. A woman was considered the responsibility, and almost the ''property,'' of her father, who then ''gave her away'' to a husband when she married. At that point, the husband had total legal authority and almost all other authority over his wife. She could not vote — until 1918 — or even own property.

In an arranged marriage, such as was prevalent in the Far East until fairly recently, the bride literally was given to her husband by her father, who had handpicked and approved the groom.

Today, a bride who keeps the traditional ''giving away'' by her father in the ceremony usually sees it as a symbol of a father's protection being exchanged for a husband's love and protection. Some ceremonies have both father and mother ''give away'' the bride, and in some, the bride gives herself away.

The bride's trousseau: The word *trousseau* comes from the French word *trousse*, which means a ''bundle.'' The bride's ''bundle'' used to contain all of her clothing and possessions which she was bringing with her to her new home. In more affluent families, this took the form of a bridal chest, or chests. At one point, a *trousseau* meant a special set of new clothing with which a well-prepared bride was outfitted, from lingerie to outer coats or cloaks and shoes. It could be very elaborate or consist of only a few pieces of apparel.

Today, the *trousseau* usually means all of the new things of dress and household goods that mark the beginning of a home.

Wedding cakes: The bride's cake started with the idea of wheat symbolizing fertility, and the primary hope for a new couple was to have many children, preferably sons. During Roman times, a thin loaf of bread was broken over the bride's head at the end of the wedding ceremony. During the Middle Ages in the West, the happy couple sealed their wedding with a kiss over a pile of small cakes. Today, those customs have evolved into a tiered wedding cake, usually with small bride and groom figures on top.

In Ireland, however, instead of a white cake, the cake usually is a heavy fruitcake with golden raisins, ground nuts, cherries and spices, much like a groom's cake in England and America.

In weddings elaborate enough to have a groom's cake, the cake traditionally was an iced fruitcake. Today, the groom usually just chooses his favorite cake and icing. The groom's cake is served at the reception along with the wedding cake, or it is cut and placed in small boxes for the guests to take home.

Rice or old shoes, or both: In the Far East, rice has the same symbology as wheat in the Middle East and West. Rice stands for the expectancy of always having enough food on the table. Also, in some cultures, rice is a symbol of fertility. Most people who throw rice at the participants in a modern wedding have no idea of the original meaning. They simply throw it because it is customary.

Among the ancient Israelites, an exchange of footwear was carried out as one formality in the sealing of a covenant, or contract. So the bride and groom exchanged sandals. Also, in the East, a red shoe on top of a house showed that a honeymoon was in progress.

Along with throwing handfuls of rice, some wedding guests tie old shoes and tin cans to the back of a newlywed couple's vehicle simply as a custom but also as a "good joke" to draw attention to their newlywed state. In the United States, the custom of writing on the vehicle with white paint or other substances has been added to the tradition, thus marking the getaway of the happy couple.

Instead of rice, Rumanians throw sweets and nuts at the new couple to indicate the hoped-for prosperity.

The honeymoon: The term comes from a Germanic custom in which the bride and groom drank a beverage made of fermented honey for the first month of their marriage, or until the waning of the moon. Whatever the length, the couple's time alone was considered a time of sweetness and happiness, an interlude in which to get to know one another before taking up the toils and routine of everyday life.

God might be said to have begun the custom of a honeymoon by telling Moses to excuse a newly married man from any civil or military duties: "When a man hath taken a new wife, he shall not go out to war, neither shall he be charged with any business; but he shall be free at home one year, and shall cheer up his wife which he hath taken" (Deut. 24:5).

Being carried over the threshold: Tradition says the groom carries the bride over the threshold of their new home. This custom is derived from ancient Rome where the bride was "dragged" over the threshold of her new home to figuratively show how reluctant she was to leave her father's house.

Traditions Around the World

In Africa, the bride and groom have their wrists tied together with plaited grass in some tribal rites.

In Austria, brides use myrtle, the "flower of life," as wreaths to hold the veils in place.

In Belgium, the bride of earlier days sewed her name on a special handkerchief, framed it, and handed it on to the next girl in the family to marry.

In Bermuda, a small tree is used to decorate the wedding cake and later is planted by the happy couple.

In China, red is the favorite choice for a wedding dress and other wedding decorations, and so forth. Red is considered the color of love, joy, and good fortune.

In Czechoslovakia, brides wear wreaths woven out of rosemary.

In England's small villages, the wedding party make a procession as they walk to the local church, with a child strewing flowers in the bride's path to denote that her life would be full of flowers and happiness.

In the island of Fiji, the groom traditionally gives the father of the bride a tooth of a whale, a symbol of good social standing and of riches.

In Finland, brides used to wear golden crowns and be blindfolded after the wedding.

Then all of the single women present would dance around her. Whoever she reached out and placed her crown on was expected to be the next bride.

In France, couples still drink a toast at the reception from a special cup that will be passed on to following generations.

In Germany, the bride and groom carry candles trimmed with ribbons and flowers.

In Greece, the custom of having godfathers and godmothers chosen at a child's birth still is observed. These men and women are not supposed to be related to the child, but usually are good friends of at least one of the parents. And a godfather or godmother is expected to oversee the child's spiritual development and be willing to take over the care of the child if anything happens to the parents. When a child grows up and marries, the godfather of the bride is an honored guest. Today, many times he is the best man at the wedding.

In Hawaii, many weddings are held at one of several caves carpeted by giant ferns.

In Holland, families held parties just before wedding ceremonies, and the bride and groom were placed on thrones under branches of evergreens, holding court. The branches symbolized everlasting love, and everyone present would come up to present good wishes to the couple.

In India, the brother of the groom sprinkles flower petals over the couple at the end of the ceremony. In most countries, a daughter's wedding costs parents more than a son's. However, in India, a daughter's wedding is *much* more expensive than a son's. Indian parents still are expected to provide a big settlement in cash and other gifts for the groom — recompense for taking responsibility for their daughter.[2]

In Iran, the Persia of ancient times, the wedding dress was yards and yards of sheeting bought by the groom and wrapped around the bride!

In Italy, confetti is thrown after the bride instead of rice; however, this confetti is sugared almonds. In England, when one bride's father learned confetti was banned at the church where his daughter was to be married, he came up with a unique alternative. He cultivated butterflies in a spare room of his home for a year before the ceremony and released 2,000 of them on the church steps after the wedding.[3]

In Korea, the groom arrives at the home of the bride on a white pony, carrying a gray goose and gander. This pair of poultry mate for life and are considered good omens of fertility.

In Mexico, wedding guests make a heart-shaped circle around the couple.

In The Philippines, a white silk cord draped around the bride and groom signifies that they are joined in an everlasting union.

In Poland, guests "buy" a dance with the bride by pinning money on her gown, a tactful way of giving money to the couple just starting out in life.

In Russia, the bride and groom give presents to the guests, as well as receive presents from them.

In Scotland, a silver teaspoon engraved with the couple's initials and date of the wedding used to be presented to the bride by the bridegroom.

In Switzerland, one of the bridesmaids leads the wedding procession to the place for the reception and hands out colored handkerchiefs to the guests, who contribute coins toward the bride's "nestegg."

In Wales, the plant myrtle shows up again. A bride gives pieces from her wedding bouquet to the bridesmaids. If the cutting lives and blooms, that is supposed to indicate a wedding for that person.

Customs and traditions make a continuity between the past and the future. They are not neccessary, of course, but most couples would have a sense of something missing, something not quite complete, without at least some of these things that have memorialized weddings for hundreds of years.

---

[1]Some of the information in this article was derived or adapted from *The Bride's Book of Etiquette* (New York: Perigee Books, The Putnam Publishing Group, 1989).

[2]Tan, Paul Lee. *Encyclopedia of 7700 Illustrations* (Rockville: Assurance Publishers, 1979), #3308, ''The Daughter in India,'' p. 779.

[3]Ibid. #3319, ''Butterflies for Confetti,'' p. 781.

The Topical Bible Gift Series
The Mother's Topical Bible
The Father's Topical Bible
The Teen's Topical Bible
The Businessman's Topical Bible
Our Life Together
Dare To Succeed

Available from your local bookstore or from:
HONOR BOOKS • P.O. Box 55388 • Tulsa, OK 74155